And When We
Pray

Suggestions and Prayers for Living in Spririt

Olive Rose Steele

Book Cover Design and Photography by Sharon Steele

Published in 2009

Distributed by
Blackwood

Library and Archives Canada Cataloguing in Publication
Steele, Olive Rose
And when we pray : suggestions and prayers for living
in spirit / Olive Rose Steele
Includes bibliographical references
ISBN 978-0-9810723-0-2
1. Prayer. I. Title.
BV210.3.S768 2008 248.3'2 C2008-908026-2

Printed in USA

I dedicate this book to my grandmother:
Eugenia Beatrice Brown (1906-1992)

❧

And to my grandmother's mother, Caroline Lawrence,
who is my guardian angel.
I honour the spiritual tract that runs through me.
May the souls of my relatives rest in peace.

For:

Mavis Adassa Wright
Sharon Lee Steele, PhD
Jessica Hope Laing
Gabriella Faith Laing

Forward

I was introduced to Olive Rose Steele nearly two decades ago by a mutual friend as the president and CEO of a successful staffing agency, situated in the heart of the business district in Toronto, Ontario.

Since that time, I have had the pleasure of working with Olive in several volunteer situations, notably along side her as senior vice president of a national association, while she was the president.

I have followed Olive's career as a business woman and as an ardent volunteer and even though I spent many hours with her, I really never knew about the spiritual aspect of her life until I became aware of her book: *And When We Pray.*

Olive loves people. She gives of herself without counting the cost. I can attest to mentoring and support that others and I have received from her.

By writing *And When We Pray,* Olive is attempting to show how we can use prayer as an added spiritual tool to help in coping with some of today's challenges. She speaks from the heart and therefore, everything she writes is from the heart.

It is my hope that her readers will be encouraged to make prayer a regular life exercise.

—Nzinga Walker

Contents

Acknowledgement

To my daughter, Sharon, I really appreciate your words of encouragement. I acknowledge my son and my beautiful granddaughters; I am a very proud grandmother.

I love you, Jessica.

I love you, Gabriella.

Grateful thanks to Rev. Cannon Donald Langdon for sharing his thoughts on angels and to Rev. Eleanor Scarlett for her thoughtfulness and encouragement.

I appreciate the support of everyone who told me it was time to share my prayers.

To my sister, Patricia Comrie: thank you for being the friend who never judges me even in those times when I messed up. And to my friend Ella Devani: you believe that I can.

The books and authors quoted in And When We Pray helped to nourish my spiritual growth and development. I hereby acknowledge these inspired authors whose writings were divinely placed in my path.

Blessings.

Introduction

SOMEONE ASKED: "Are you a Christian?" As I recall, I was sitting in a crammed underground train, unaware of anyone around me, until I heard the question being asked of no one in particular. I remember being preoccupied with a nagging sense that I was about to lose another business contract. I just could not shake the knot in my belly—I was in no mood to listen to a subway sermon.

The Scriptures have always been my reference. I never felt I had to have religion in order to receive God's blessings. I never thought I needed to be "saved" and be "born again", for that matter, to reach out in prayer. I truly believed that approaching God is about having a spiritual state of mind.

I rejected the view that God is a demanding jealous master who requires His children (servants) to admit to being born in sin and having to confess and repent of these sins in order to fulfill their spiritual self. My attitude is that God, our Heavenly Father, is generous and giving and all that is required of me is to communicate my wishes in prayer.

In this book, *And When We Pray*, I put across my point of view on the basis of my complete confidence and belief in the wisdom that created me.

In some of my most difficult, awkward moments I prayed that God would use me as an instrument of his love, in any and every way, to reach as many of his children as possible. These prayers were said from a fearful, selfish bargaining stance with hopes of receiving a quick miracle.

In my heart, I knew I would renege on any deal I made with God. I was taken aback when I was called to be true to the words I said during prayers. My self-imposed insignificance would not be accepted by the Divine as a bargaining chit or a way for not heeding the call.

My surrender and my brokenness; my fears and my disappointments; my ups and downs; and all of my dreaded negative thoughts are presented in *And When We Pray* to encourage others to use prayer as a helpful spiritual tool.

The core of *And When We Pray* is my prayer practice, my personal relationship with God, my relationship with those whom I come in daily contact and my appreciation of answered prayers.

In *And When We Pray*, I integrate my own life story with suggestions and prayers to show how we can link the pieces of our experiences to learn life's lessons.

The prayers in *And When We Pray* may be useful to those who are attending worship and those interested in exploring ways to inner peace.

It is my hope that *And When We Pray* will aid in your prayer practice and even assist you in fashioning your own prayers.

Once again, I ask my readers to accept my writing style as my way of expressing my knowledge and understanding of my spiritual self. I am reminded of the first stanza of a sacred children's poem as follows:

> "Gentle Jesus, meek and mild, Look upon a little
> child, Pity my simplicity, Suffer me to come to thee,"
> Charles Wesley.

I welcome your feedback:

Blackwood
4 Robert Speck Parkway
Suite 1500, Mississauga
Ontario Canada
L4Z 1S1

Opening Prayer

Dear God,
With hands clasped, we enter Your Light
We leave at the door everything we believe to be right
We confess all negative thoughts and feelings
We embrace Your Divine Spirit within us
Purify our hearts and renew our spirits
Give us understanding, peace and love
Show mercy and heal our spiritual and physical pain
Shine Your White Light upon us, Dear God
And Illuminate our consciousness
As we seek refuge in this special place
Amen

One
What is Prayer?

PRAYER IS AN ACT of spontaneous outpourings from the heart with faith in the Invisible Force that sustains life, to provide that for which we pray. Prayer is communicating that we are ready to manifest our wishes and desires in human form. When we pray we are demonstrating our belief in a power that is greater than our own. Completely trusting that our prayer requests will be manifested makes us independent of the opinions and advice of others.

"I pray for calm and inner peace," "I pray because it is an obligation and a necessity," "I pray for my needs," "I pray for my family and their needs," "I pray when I am worried," and "I pray for a miracle" are some reasons why people pray.

Every thought, every word and every activity is a prayer. We live our prayers. Sometimes we mumble and affirm passages without paying attention to outcomes and we beg and plead without taking into account affect and consequences. Know that mumblings and pleadings are far from meaningless for if they come from the heart they are, in fact, prayers.

Since we live and move in a perpetual state of prayer then we should pay close attention to our thoughts, our words, our actions and our way of life.

Consciously blessing those who would do us harm; meditating on the plight of individuals in lesser circumstances; being mindful of our own blessings; and spending time alone in silent contemplation will keep us in sync with what some people say is our "higher self".

We have a tendency to identify and talk about our life based on our experiences, judgments, opinions and ideas and rightly so, because our experiences are what we know about ourselves. We really don't have to validate what we already know, although what we think we know about ourselves may not necessarily be our entire truth. Many will agree that there is more to us than meet the eye. The question is: what is more?

For me, more is accepting that I am a living, breathing spiritual manifestation of a Divine Plan. More is the knowledge that I am an integral part of that Plan. More is knowing that as part of the Divine Plan, I live and move with freedom to be myself. Acknowledging that I am truly more than the form I took at birth assists my spiritual growth.

While it is true that our core spiritual need is to share the deepest part of our soul without being judged, many of us are not convinced that prayer is the answer. We often pray with doubt that our prayers will have a positive outcome and we are inclined to only accept outcomes that match our needs. Whether our needs lead us to pray for others or to plead our own case, it is always a good idea to spend part of our prayer time giving thanks. When we give thanks for family, friends, good health, a job, food, shelter and clothing, we change the tone of our prayers in a positive way.

The foundation of my prayers is my worth. Do I deserve the blessings for which I ask? How hard should I bargain? Should I plead my case with tears?

In the midst of some of my doubtful moments I prayed to be blessed with plenty, all the time believing that God only listens to the prayers of those who already have abundance.

I have been told to quit praying for more because it is possible that I already received all that I am ever going to have in this life. Nevertheless, I never doubted that my prayers could be beneficial to others and for that reason it was difficult for me to accept that I am already all I ever will be.

> *"Surely goodness and mercy shall follow me all the days of my life," Psalm 23:6.*

Very often I meditate on blessings I expect to receive and I give thanks in advance for these blessings to be manifested in my life in perfect ways. Giving thanks reminds me of the good I already enjoy and encourages me to ask for more.

During some of my egotistical moments, I lost things and broke things; I felt abandoned and unloved, neglected and persecuted; I harboured doubt and fear; and I became angry and resentful for no logical reason. I often cursed every piece of literature that says God is generous and good.

> *"He shall receive the blessing from the Lord, and righteousness from the God of his salvation," Psalms: 24:5.*

> *"And he shall be like a tree planted by the rivers of water, that bringeth forth his fruit in his season; his leaf also shall not wither; and whatsoever he doeth shall prosper," Psalms: 1: 3.*

Life's challenges come and go, always in flux, and therefore problems that are to be expected should, in fact, not be taken personally.

We may deny some situations just to keep our sanity or we may say "this too shall pass" but we really should not allow a negative state of affairs to linger too long. Always try to remember the times when things were in sync and you were happy, healthy and prosperous.

You are your moments. Delight in their complexities. Know that we choose and decide which situations we want to savor and which ones we want to discard.

When you pray, be unwavering, believing that your prayers will manifest in the moment you pray. Faith in your thoughts and words is your confidence that all of your needs will be met according to your riches. I call this unwavering belief our "*Built in Prayer Mechanism*" in motion.

Our prayers live and breathe because of the life we put into them. Approach your prayers like having a never-ending conversation with a listener who is only a breath away.

I have experienced miracles that I know is as a result of my confidence in my prayers.

I pray to relieve my stresses, calm my fears and heal my physical and spiritual pain. Prayer is my remedy for everything that ails me. And when we put our trust in our prayers, it seems like new and more difficult challenges emerge in our life. Know that these challenges do not belong to us; they are of this world and we are not of this world.

Two
Prayer Practice

"People who have developed a firm faith, grounded in understanding and rooted in daily practice, are in general much better at coping with adversity than those who have not,"
His Holiness The Dalai Lama

PRACTICES SUCH AS daily prayers and meditation can be beneficial to everyone and such practices should not necessarily be attached to particular religious beliefs. Pray under any and all circumstances and God will answer.

I sometimes question my embrace of God's Spirit that I know is within and I often doubted my spiritual connection to Grace. But any doubt I may have soon erased as I meditate on God's unconditional love.

Like many, I have reacted to the challenges of coping with today's living and the state of our world with instant short prayers, such as: "Lord, have mercy," "God help us," "Oh my God," and so on. We don't consider these responses prayers but they are. I call them "prayers on the run".

We say these responses in a rush and when we reach to the

point where we are genuinely exhausted by life's stresses and tired of dealing with the never ending day to day annoyances, we turn to prayer as an alternative way of coping.

In trying to cope with my own annoyances, I trip and fall on myself. Translation—I make mistakes. But with every supposed mistake my faith grew stronger.

Stress happens. It's how we handle those states of affairs that matter to us. Lest we forget, stress causes hypertension, depression, attacks our heart and brings on cancerous dis-ease. And when we are stressed, we are tempted to seek relief through a variety of good and not so good habits.

Our individual challenges are different and many times we would rather keep our own stresses than experience the next person's worries. When we tumble into stressful situations, we feel we are experiencing the worse times of our life.

Very often negative thoughts and feelings of hopelessness caused me to give up on ideas and dreams that I knew would work for my good. My big ego is my worst enemy.

Know that our Heavenly Father is acquainted with each and every one of us and He promises to help in our times of need.

> *"...Nevertheless I am not ashamed: for I know whom I believe, and I am persuaded that he is able to keep that which I have committed unto him against that day," To Timothy, 1:12.*

I consider that instead of becoming addicted to worldly remedies to survive any unhappiness I ran into, I would choose the spiritual alternative of prayer for relieving pain and negative emotions. I soon developed the habit of praying regularly, all the time remembering God's promise to keep his eye on us.

"Behold, the eye of the Lord is upon them that fear him, upon them that hope in his mercy," Psalms: 33: 18.

"Yea, though I walk through the valley of the shadow of death, I will fear no evil: for thou art with me," Psalm 23:4.

"Fear thou not: for I am with thee: be not dismayed; for I am thy God: I will strengthen thee; yea I will help thee; yea I will uphold thee with the right hand of my righteousness," Isaiah 41:10.

Amazing things happen in our hearts when we pray. To start with, we are able to get beyond hurtful feelings, hardened jealously and the fear of abandonment. As we release our fears in prayer we begin to trust in God's unconditional love and we forgive and even forget some negative practices that once stood in our way and move forward with optimism.

It is not all bad to display lack of enthusiasm from time to time, since it becomes necessary, on occasions, to give consideration and expression to some worrisome situations. I say, embrace the negative thoughts, be with your feelings, and then release every thought that is not of love. This is not an easy task, but every one of us is capable.

Many times, after I have prayed, I am prompted to call on specific individuals. Quite often, my visits turned out to be the answer to someone's prayer. You see, God relies on us to speak lovingly to those who might be feeling unloved or abandoned or in despair. He uses us as a conduit to connect and bless others.

"Don't sweat what comes through. If it feels like you're on target, try it. God would never inspire you to do something hurtful or dangerous," Barbara Y. Martin with Dimitri Moralitis.

No matter the situation, when you are weighted down by your own cares, earnestly pray for other individuals. Make loving requests on behalf of the hungry, the friendless, those who are sick, those who may have done you wrong, those who have not shown you love and those who you would not have recognized except when you kneel in prayer. Pray for others and notice how light your own burden becomes. Ask for God's mercy upon others and see how clearer your thoughts appear.

> *"Thou shall not avenge, nor bear any grudge against the children of thy people, but thou shall love thy neighbor as thyself," Leviticus: 19:18*

> *"And when ye stand praying, forgive, if ye have ought against any, that your Father also which is in heaven may forgive your trespasses. But if ye do not forgive, neither will your Father which is in heaven forgive your trespasses," Mark 11: 25-26*

It is probably easier for many of us to profess love for our neighbours than to truly accept and love ourselves.

It was challenging for me to be gentle and loving to me because I never accepted that I am whole and perfect. It was difficult to forgive me when I messed up and it was very difficult to accept that God loves me in my present state and all that I am likely to become. I constantly "beat up" on myself in my struggle to achieve perfect happiness.

No matter the situation, whenever you find yourselves confused, anxious, angry, jealous, fearful, and feeling tormented, trust in the Divine and watch the situation settle down. We can go to that quiet place in our heart where God says, "Come unto me" and know that there is no limit to our requests. God's plan is for our personal and intimate communication with Him so that we may experience love, joy, peace and healing.

Three
Why We Pray

"God is in the midst of her, she shall not be moved God shall help her, and that right early," Psalms 46:5.

WE SEEK SPIRITUAL meaning in our life. Deep down we want to believe that we are part of a bigger scheme, a scheme that allows us to live in a world of perfect health and prosperity. And since our desire is to stay in our physical state for a long time, we seek out priests, pastors, imams, spiritualists, psychics, fitness programs and diets; anyone and anything that ensures our longer life.

My desire for spiritual knowledge started at a very young age. In Sunday School, I was taught bible verses, which I now recite in moments of stress. The "Sankeys" I sang at the feet of my grandmother, I now hum softly in meditative reflections. Unimportant is what I call myself. Truth is, affluent and rich is really what I am, even though my earthly lineage and my personality keeps reminding me of all the reasons I would be unwise to call myself affluent or even rich.

A colleague said to me once: "You will be a wealthy woman". I responded that I already felt "wealthy", for in my mind, I was enjoying the wealth and successes of life.

For no apparent reasons, and without warning, everything I thought I was enjoying came to a screeching halt. My supposed wealth and successes began to unravel. I quickly fell to my knees in prayer with hopes that my situation would turn around quickly, before I was exposed.

I hunkered down in denial and disbelief. God abandoned me. I became confused and angry. Fear set in. I concluded I was being punished for something I had done wrong. I was not making sense.

In the middle of my confusion and fear, I was literally blinded by tearful outbursts. I bargained with God. I said if He planted my feet back on sold ground; if I recovered the things I lost, if I bounced back lickety-split, I would be more frugal. Things got better for a short time then I fell headlong into several of what some people call "valley" situations" and I stayed in them much too long.

What is a valley? Valleys are low and uncomfortable points in our life. They are stagnant unfamiliar places where we sometimes find ourselves with no idea how to exit. I call my valleys "pit stops".

Negative thoughts and emotions, fear, jealousy, hate and bad judgment always plunged me into valleys.

When I find myself in a valley, I step back and view the situation as an onlooker would—with an open mind. It is when I "*Cast my burden on the Christ within,*" *Florence Scovel-Shinn.*

Dear God,
I am sitting in a lonely valley
Hemmed beneath a high mountain
This place is strange and uncomfortable
I cannot remember when or even how I got here

Shine a light in this cold and desolate place
Help me to find my way out
Give me the strength to endure as I claw my way to safety
I now cast this burden on the Christ within
And wait for my miracle
In Jesus name Amen

Valley situations demand Divine intervention.

Valley situations make you crazy.

Picture yourself in a valley, alone; you remain quiet, silently shameful. Those you love express loss of faith in your judgment. They say you must be irresponsible to have put yourself in such a rut. You change the conversation when friends and associates inquire how things are going with you. You show courage though; you insist things are going good. But you know it would be foolish of you to admit that your car has just been repossessed or your partner left you for someone else or you have been evicted from your apartment. You sweat your prayers. You ask God to come to your rescue before someone carts you off to the nut house. Sounds familiar? I know that feeling.

> *"For I know the thoughts that I think towards you,*
> *saith the Lord, thoughts of peace, and not of evil to*
> *give you an expected end," Jeremiah 29:11-13*

At some of my low points, prayers hit or miss. My spiritual ignorance made me pray that God would supply just enough to take care of my basic day-to-day needs. Still, shortages were the order of the day. It was difficult for me to accept that those outward appearances were the outgrowths of my own input.

I remained stubborn and steadfast, always wallowing in my dramatics. Going from one project to the next; engaging in fruitless activities to mask my true feelings; inappropriately blaming everyone and everything for the cause of my imaginary failures, all the while telling God that He moves much too slow for my liking.

We force our way through our challenges because we believe we are in control; we try to fix things, no matter how things have gotten worse under our management. We say we are in control, no matter that we continue to lose things, break things and struggle to keep things.

Some of our troubles in life may very well be as a result of our violation of Universal Laws. For example, when we are kind to others, others are kind to us in return. Based on my own experiences, I would say that when we are happy, healthy and prosperous, and everything is going well, we sometimes become puffed-up, haughty and unappreciative.

The only power that is worth having is the power of the love of God. He continuously directs and guides us no matter that we often times forget that we are not truly in control.

We will experience tough times at points in our life. Like me, you may feel ashamed to acknowledge that your plans did not turn out to your liking. You may be too proud to open your heart to your closest friend about your supposed failure.

So your project didn't produce your desired results; your business partner had different ideas from you about the business; and your spouse showed you that no one is perfect. What do you do? Pick yourself up, brush the dust off and begin again. Unless we have experienced the not so good side to our life, we will not fully understand and even appreciate the good side.

Situations that are beyond our control and situations that we cannot fix make us feel guilty. I suggest you give over everything that burdens you to the Christ in you. God always reveal the perfect way out. He is never late. Learn from your experiences and move on.

> *"Yea, let none that wait on thee be ashamed,"*
> *Psalms 25:3.*

> *"They Looked unto Him, and were lightened: and their faces were not ashamed," Psalms 34:5*

Spouses, relatives, friends, and well-meaning individuals are usually supportive and sympathetic about your struggles but they may have problems of their own. They will say encouraging and reassuring words as they watch you go through your personal worries. They will tell you that God is testing you. You will ask, "Why me?"

The song says: "*O what needless pain we bear, all because we do not carry everything to God in prayer.*"

Quite often, my ego calls up my greatest fear: poverty. This fear stalks me in the form of ruthless debt collectors; it haunts me in a recurring dream in which I am walking to school wearing flip flops while my classmates dressed in shoes and socks. With this fear of poverty comes the fear of losing credibility; the fear of not being loved and, for some unknown reason, the fear of experiencing poor health. These fears are powerful.

> *"Every experience is ordered by Grace to teach and remind us of who we are in the Divine scheme of things," Iyanla Vansant.*

There is no way I could have known that the lessons I learnt as Spirit unfold would provide me with personal and first hand knowledge about my incredible life journey. My testimony about the unlimited love of God, and His help whenever I call is my proof that His love is the greatest gift.

The God I fear is gentle and loving. He lives in the heart of everyone; He is everywhere and in everything. "*For in Him we live and move and have our being,*" *Acts 17:28*

But this has not always been the case: understand that I grew up with a false belief that I should be fearful of God because I am sinful and deserving of punishment for my sins. Remembering the horrible death that Jesus Christ suffered for "my sins" always makes me sad. In my mind, there is no way that I should deserve God's forgiveness and unconditional love.

The idea that God's love makes me breathe puts me to sleep and wakes me up each day is overwhelming to me. And when I revert to my old ways of thinking and believing as I sometimes do, I call to mind God's unconditional love and know that it is wherever I may find myself.

Four

When You Pray

"When you pray you rise to meet in the air those who are praying in that very hour, and whom save in prayer you may not have met," The Prophet, Kahlil Gibran.

"But thou, when thou prayest, enter into thy closet, and when thou hast shut thy door, pray to the father which is in secret; and the father which seeith in secret shall reward thee openly," Matthew 6:6.

THE LORD'S PRAYER is recorded in Matthew 6: 9-13 as follows:

> *Our father which art in heaven, Hallowed be thy name. Thy kingdom come, thy will be done in earth, as it is in heaven. Give us this day our daily bread. And forgive us our debts, as we forgive our debtors. And lead us not into temptation, but deliver us from evil. For thine is the kingdom and the power and the glory for ever and ever. Amen*

The Psalmist David penned some very powerful prayers. Individuals, down through the ages, recorded and left passionate prayers which many of us repeat for our daily spiritual needs. The peace prayer of St. Francis of Assisi reminds me that my spiritual growth will not be a fast and easy affair:

> *Lord make me an instrument of Your peace; Where there is hatred, let me sow love; Where there is injury, pardon; Where there is error, the truth; Where there is doubt, the faith; Where there is despair, hope; Where there is darkness, light; Where there is sadness, joy. O Divine Master; Grant that I may not so much seek; To be consoled, as to console; To be understood, as to understand; To be loved, as to love. For it is in giving that we receive; It is in pardoning, that we are pardoned; It is in dying that we are born to eternal life.*

It seems to me that when we pray we call upon a Higher Power. We believe that there is some "Thing", within and without, which is greater and more powerful.

When I say: "*Our Father Who art in Heaven, hallowed be thy name,*" I am calling on a Father that supersedes every other father that I may be familiar with. I am praising and adoring my Heavenly Father; I am giving thanks to God whom I call Father, Creator of everything, known and unknown. It is therefore right that we begin our prayers in praise and recognition of our Divine Heavenly Father.

The challenge for me is whether to pray aloud, intimately whispering or reclining in meditative contemplation. I do believe the act of praying to be personal and private and so I tend to pray quietly, often in meditative contemplation. As I mature and grow spiritually, I see myself as I truly am: a child of God needing unconditional love, wishing to reach higher spiritual heights and praying as Spirit leads.

My prayers are my expressions and my feelings; they are the

inside of my soul laid bare before my Heavenly Father; they are conversations from my heart and many were said during challenges that placed me between a rock and a hard place. But the peace, joy and comfort I experienced after every expression of prayer is beyond my explanation.

There were times when I bargained with God and made promises that God already knew I could not keep. Regardless, God answered every prayer and even though I ignored some answers because they did not match what I expected, I knew that God's plans for me took precedence over my own plans and expectations.

God, our heavenly Father, always gives us all that is good and right for us.

No person prays better than another and no person is "called" or knows the "right" ways to pray. I don't believe there has to be a special place to go to pray or that there should be set numbers of prayers to be repeated at particular times of the day or night. Our prayers are our immediate and direct connection with the Divine.

I tend to agree with author David Kuntz: *"Prayer is simply an attitude of the heart that desires communication with the Divine."*

And when I pray, *"Thy Will be done on earth as it is in Heaven"*, I am calling for love, peace and happiness which is our perfect gift and which is God's promise to everyone.

When you repeat the Lord's Prayer, wrap your thoughts around each word with feelings. Claim the meaning of each phrase with confidence and with no second thought.

Let your words flow:

> *"Let the words of my mouth and the meditation of my heart be acceptable in thy sight, of Lord my strength and my redeemer,"* Psalms 19:14

"That if we ask anything according to His will, He hears us," 1 John 5: 14.

Our prayer meetings with the Divine should be in earnest, bearing in mind we don't always know what is good for us. Neither do we know what is good for others.

Everyone, at some point, prayed for things, prayed over things, prayed because things happened and prayed in intercession for others. Prayer puts us in a personal relationship with God.

"The method by which you may communicate with infinite intelligence is very similar to that through which the vibration of sound is communicated...." Napoleon Hill.

It is a fact that people and situations have changed because of prayers. Whether you were taught at an early age to pray or you learnt this rite later as you mature, or, like so many people, circumstances propelled you to speak your heart to comfort your soul, sooner or later we will express ourselves in prayerful ways.

People have experienced miracles through intercessory prayers; others have witnessed miracles as a result of their own pleadings.

But whether we pray on bended knees, by the side of our bed, in houses of worship, in quiet affirmations or aloud, how we pray, when and why we pray reflects our understanding of your personal relationship with God.

"I do not ask you to meditate or pray for an hour a day, although there is nothing wrong with this. I simply ask you to remember your Devine Essence for five minutes out of each hour, or for one thought out of every ten", Paul Farrini.

I used to pray only when I found myself in a jam or when there was an emergency in my life. The quick "Lord have mercy" would be all that I thought I needed.

When I did not recognize the answers to my prayers, I looked back on my state of mind in the very moment I prayed. Was I blaming my history for my present shortcomings? Was I confused, fearful, doubtful, angry, jealous, and resentful? Did I honestly empty my heart of negative thoughts? Was I holding on to old grief, hurt and pitiful wounds?

We can be assured that when we go to God in prayer, having nothing in our hands, with no agenda and no set outcomes, we will recognize our answers. In due time the answers we expected will be same as the answers we received.

> *"The purpose of prayer is the alignment of the mind with the thoughts and the will of God," Marianne Williamson.*

> *"It is never too late to turn to God and say: 'God. My answer has filled my mind with fear. My answer has brought only pain and struggle into my life. It must be the wrong answer. Will you please help me to find another one?'" Paul Farrini.*

Entertain quietness and feel life. Feel the Spirit wherever you are, know that God is with you in your simplest or your most triumphant experiences.

I lost my way to a meeting because I exited the bus too soon. From where I stood I could see the building that my meeting was being held, however, a wide road separated me. Vehicles whizzed past. I was scared to attempt a crossing. I literally stood still, my brief case in my right hand, my heart in my throat. It seemed I stood still for a long time but on reflection, it had been only seconds. I turned and walked toward a safe spot by the side of the road and suddenly, from out of nowhere, a cab pulled up beside me. I pointed to where I intended to go. He beckoned me to hop in. In less than three minutes, I was at my destination.

Now I am not one who readily confers blessings, however, on exiting the cab I said to the driver, "God Bless You". To my surprise he replied, "My name is Terry, mention me when you pray."

Always remember, a thought is a prayer.

Know that your prayers are answered with your permission. By that I mean we consciously or unconsciously created the space in our heart and the conditions in our life for our prayers to be answered. We surrendered all outcomes. We gave up control and we accepted the flow of the Spirit. God our Father does the rest.

> *"He shall call upon me, and I will answer him: I will be with him in trouble; I will deliver him, and honor him,"* Psalms 91:15.

Pray continuously. It is what we ought to do to receive everything we want and need in our life. Our *Built-in Prayer Mechanism* is always on auto-pilot.

Five

Our Built-In Prayer Mechanism

I TAKE FOR granted that we are created with an instinct that lets us cry out in times of trouble to an unseen some "One", some "Thing" or some "Sense". Here, I will admit I am not qualified to argue about religion, dogma or conviction, for that matter. I am making the point that we are spiritually "wired" to call for help from a Higher Source in moments of distress and dire need.

This *Built-in Prayer Mechanism* that I talk about stirs our beliefs and makes us have faith in times when the situation seems impossible. The tumor is diagnosed as inoperable; your chances of conceiving are nil, your spouse announced it is time to call the relationship "a day" and wants a divorce; and your out-of-control child telephones you from jail. What do you do? Be guided by your *Built-in Prayer Mechanism* as it prompts you to pray and trust the Spirit to make the outcome positive. The chorus says:

> *"It is no secret what God can do, what he's done for others He'll do for you."*

I entered a deep and challenging place. I had been praying for help. In the midst of my conversation with my higher self I recognized myself saying, "Father, my faith will not let me doubt". From within I heard a clear voice: "Hold on to your belief, your *Built-in Prayer Mechanism* will guide you in prayer".

When in doubt, I err on the side of pragmatism, however, in this instance Spirit addressed me with such directness and clarity I had to pay attention. Comforting words began to flow—my spirit reclined in the words I spoke. In that moment I knew that life can only be good. I was at peace.

It is truly reassuring to know that God has given each and every one of us everything we need to survive.

> *"If you go into business, --and most of us are in business of some sort or another, or you enter into an undertaking of some kind, you equip it. You equip it with everything you think it will need... and you expect it to function well. That is what God did with us," Mildred Man.*

Since we were born with everything we need to sustain us in this life, then our birthright guarantees us perfect health, wealth and fulfillment.

I am convinced that God, our Mother, did not birth us to live, suffer and die. We have to believe that our blessings come with our name written on them and our blessings will never go to any one else.

But we are not always sure of what we want so we don't recognize our blessings when they appear.

On many occasions, out of feelings of unworthiness, I settled for less than I desired, mainly because of the conditions I placed on myself. When you know what you want, then ask for it with confidence, accept nothing less.

All of us should spiritually develop to the point where we are able to manifest our blessings, through faith. The course of action is reliance on our *Built-in Prayer Mechanism,* which is available to help us form a personal relationship with God.

In some of my prayers I use the sentence, "Because I ask, I must receive." The fact that I am seeking a blessing means that the blessing is seeking me; therefore, I pray for a clear path to receiving good things.

Circumstances make us forget our rights and privileges. We break stuff, we lose stuff, we find stuff, we want and need stuff; and we are scared because stuff we don't like happens. These circumstances will plunge us into spiritual negativity. I call it fear. In between the negatives, our magnificent *Built-in Prayer Mechanism* will take over. Just allow it.

I marvel when I think that God loves me not because of anything special that I have done or will ever do but because I am perfect in his eyes.

A friend of mine told me I was conceited to actually believe I am perfect in God eyes. I responded to the contrary. I told her it was, in fact, very humbling to know that I and everyone of God's children are perfect in His eyes. We only have to believe this to be true.

Steadfast belief in our *Built-in Prayer Mechanism* will activate Divine power within us and lift our spirits to a higher faith at the right moment. It is never arrogant to acknowledge the Divine Spirit within us and our inherited place in the eyes of God.

We sometimes see negative circumstances as unanswered prayers and we may observe the situation with a: "God, I did not ask for this". Know that a "Why me?" moment is a moment for learning.

Psalm 23:

*The Lord is my Sheppard; I shall not want;
He maketh me to lie down in green pastures; He
leadeth me beside the still waters; He restoreth my
soul; He leadeth me in the paths of righteousness
for his name's sake. Yea, though I walk through the
valley of the shadow of death, I will fear no evil for
thou art with me; thy rod and thy staff they comfort me. Thou preparest a table before me in the
presence of mine enemies; thou anointest my head
with oil; my cup runneth over. Surely goodness and
mercy shall follow me all the days of my life; and I
will dwell in the house of the Lord forever.*

The 23rd Psalm assures us that the Lord our God has already
taken care of every possible occurrence that will confront us.

I am tough on me when I don't see the answers to my prayers
in real time. My ego thoughts remind me of my sinful self and I
judge myself harshly. But afterwards I back-up. I reflect on past
challenges and I thank God for bringing me through those past
challenges—challenges that literally broke my heart.

In those times, when the road ahead seems dark and winding,
my senses assure me that I am on the right track. Those are times
when my words, though muffled, resound on a higher level.

I usually begin my prayers by thanking God for a new day. Just
to wake up and inhale the first gasp of fresh air each day is a privilege. And to experience the good and the not so good things in the
moment is a lesson to be learnt in the school of life.

The songwriter says: "*What a privilege to carry, everything to
God in prayer*".

Six
Simple Prayers

"NOW I LAY me down to sleep; I pray the Lord my soul to keep, And if I die before I wake; I pray the lord my soul to take, Author unknown, is probably the first prayer many children, including my own grandchildren learnt. But if you look closely at this prayer you will observe a prayer about life on earth, faith in the Creator and a belief in eternal life. It is about placing our life into the hands of an all powerful Source with faith that our eyes will open and close in restful sleep from day to day, and when our eyes close in final rest, our spirit continues into eternity.

When our prayers are simple and uncomplicated everything we do turns out easy and effortless.

The coupon I held in my hand was specifically to be traded for a free donut. My mind was made up before I entered the coffee shop that I was going to be as dramatic as I could about asking to have my donut coupon substituted for a cup of coffee. I wanted coffee and I see no reason that a donut coupon with the same value could not be traded for a cup of coffee.

The attendant in this particular coffee shop strictly obeyed the rule: donut coupons were to be exchanged for donuts and coffee coupons were to be exchanged for coffee. No amount of drama on my part or anyone else, for that matter, would bend or sway the rules. I should have kept it simple and done the obvious.

Very often we pray with drama similar to my donut incident. We make tearful requests in doubt and fear and we complain that God never answers our prayers. I say, surrender to peacefulness, embrace order and experience ease with simplicity every time.

> *"We cannot ask thee for aught, for thou knowest our needs before they are born in us: Thou art our need; and in giving us more of thyself thou givest us all," Kahlil Gibran.*

And because every one of us is connected to the one Source, which is God; and He knows what is in our heart then we should say our burning desires and say them with simplicity so that our requests will be manifested according to our will.

> *"For the Lord seeth not as man seeth: for man looketh on the outward appearance, but the Lord looketh on the heart," 1Samuel 16:7.*

I know a woman who dedicated much of her time to "interviewing" men with whom she formed a relationship, in her quest to find a "Mr. Right". Just as she gave up trying to find this perfect gentleman a miracle happened.

Her story is: she was feeling abandoned, lonely and unloved; and minding her own business on the day her man asked her to be his wife. One could be tempted to disbelieve her account of the marriage proposal but that was truly how it happened. Mind you, at that point in her life, she had changed her prayer request to finding a partner "to keep her company," a lesser demand, when compared to the previous years of praying outright for "Mr. Right", her perfect husband.

Her prayer was answered in a big way; he was, in fact, everything she prayed for. I told her she was a lucky woman and I meant it. I believe God is the giver and God is the Gift.

Those who pray for a "right" person to be manifested in their life should be careful in making such prayer requests. I suggest that you be right for yourself before you pray for someone to be right for you. Know that we attract our mirror images. We should not forget that God created only one right and perfect Son, Our Lord Jesus Christ, and He loves us all. Every other son and daughter comes with the same ego-based flaws. Therefore, we should learn to love each other as God loves us and we should refuse to entertain the idea that there is a special love "out there" that we ought to actively pursue.

Learning to love and accept ourselves as beings, made in God's likeness, regardless of how we may perceive ourselves, assists us and facilitates the development of our spiritual form. And so, as our awareness evolves and we embrace ourselves as loving individuals, we are obliged to also accept our sisters and brothers in the same manner.

Our individual viewpoints and ideas about the use of prayers are less important when compared with the benefits of this habit on the human psyche. I say be confident when you pray and keep the practice of praying simple. Always be mindful that uncertainties and worries will crop up in our life. Incorporate strength and courage with your confidence and *"Wait on the Lord,"*. *Psalms 27:14.*

Seven
Pray the Psalms

"Let the word of Christ dwell in you richly in all wisdom; teaching and admonishing one another in Psalms and hymns and spiritual songs, singing with grace in your hearts to the lord,". Colossians 3:16.

WARM AND FUZZY, cold and hurtful, broken and contrite, it is all there to recite from the Psalms. I have dropped to my knees umpteen times to recite verses and passages of the Psalms and I come away every time with comforting feelings. Some Psalms speak directly to your worries and distress in the moment. I say recite them in your moment of need.

I love the Psalms. Whenever I feel hurt, pitiful and needy I open the Scriptures at a Psalm.

> *"The Lord is my rock and my fortress and my deliver; my God, my strength, in whom I will trust, my buckler and the horn of my salvation, my high tower," Psalms 18:2.*

It is true that there were times when the Psalmist David doubted his status in God's eyes, perhaps angry; very mindful of his enemies and often times not wished them well, but he never failed to express his love for the Lord in beautiful songs, worship and praise. All of us can relate the Psalms to some aspects of our modern thinking.

Over lunch one day an associate shared his objection to the anger and damnation expressed in some Psalms. His criticism is that he sees no reason for such harsh words. It was difficult for my colleague to conceive of such damning wishes on anyone including an enemy.

Remember, we are all creatures of ego and the Psalmist David was no different. The ego always encourages us to be weary of everything we cannot see, hear, feel and touch. Ego maintains that we stand up for ourselves; be in control. Ego convinces us that we should go to a higher authority when we feel threatened; a parent, if you will, and maybe the situation will be resolved. Therefore, it is not unusual for us to pray our fears. But know that when we pray fear-based prayers it is our ego once again rearing its ugly head.

Our Heavenly Father knows our individual heart. He guides and directs us through every aspect of our life and when we pray our fears; our Heavenly Father lifts us up with renewed spirits. God our Father expects us to come to Him with our fears. It is comforting to know that He hears and answers all our prayers.

Whether real or perceived, there were moments when I felt cornered and overrun by enemy thoughts. Fear of looming danger, fear of shame and humiliation, fear of losing love and admiration, fear of ill health, fear of poverty. You name it, I feared it. These fears caused me great anxiety; they gnaw me until I fell down on both knees.

And there is always a Psalms that will speak to me and subside my fears. The Psalms teach me to approach the presence of the Divine with nothing in my hand: *a broken and a contrite heart. O God, thou wilt not despise.* In those moments I pour out the contents of my heart and rise from my knees with confidence and a renewed spirit.

Within the context of how I pray, I will admit that the Psalms empower me to address the Divine Heavenly Mother in words only a child with no predetermined notions could express. I follow the example of the Psalmist David in some of my emotional prayers but I am mindful that everything we think about, wish for and utter, are prayers. I therefore implore you to pray with love in your heart.

Dear God,
Please protect my mind from lies and enemy thoughts
Help me to clearly hear your voice over any other
Shield me from misleading and destructive thinking
Where enemy thoughts are already in my mind
Help me to push them back by inviting the power of Your Divine
    Holy Spirit to cleanse my thinking
Protect my thoughts from doubt and confusion
So that I can make right and proper judgments
Have mercy upon me Dear God, and give me peace
I humbly ask these mercies in Jesus Name
Amen

It is true that the foundation of numerous prayers down the through the ages has been predicated on the Psalms. Many of us can recite a verse or two or even an entire Psalm that sets us free and gives us hope and courage to endure in moments of stress.

In some of my very challenging moments, I directed harsh prayers to sisters I believed to be trying to confine my determination and progress; brothers I perceived to be doing me some undefined wrong and people I never met I judged to hate me without a cause. Fear-based prayers have relevancy in so far as they initially soothe the ego-based human psyche; however, it would not be a spiritually healthy situation to always pray unkind and vindictive prayers.

I was feeling wronged. A certain child of God eroded my dignity. I bended two knees before my Heavenly Mother, although I had my own ideas about how I wanted the outcome of the situation to be. I knew that my ego had taken over the direction of my thoughts because fear, anger and revenge set in. My ego thoughts gave me 50 ways in which I could and should get even.

I sought the counsel of my spiritual sister. She was touched. She was always touched when I fall in a ditch and become spiritually stuck. She said, "Let us pray."

I adjusted the weight on my knees and quickly rose to my feet; I could not pray when she urged me to repeat Psalms 109. Much as I thought I was mistreated and wrongly judged I could not approach my Heavenly Mother with such hate in my heart towards a sister.

In His Sermon on the Mount as recorded in Matthew 5, Jesus Christ preached the following in verse 44:

> But I say unto you, love your enemies, bless them
> that curse you, do good to them that hate you, and
> pray for them which despitefully use you, and per-
> secute you. Matthew 5:44.

And further in verse 48:

> Be ye therefore perfect, even as your Father which is
> in heaven is perfect.

I must admit, I am still learning to forgive me for entertaining unkind thoughts, words and actions toward another. I am still learning to suspend judgment and negative opinions about others.

Everyone, believer or non-believer will find the Psalms appropriate for their everyday spiritual needs. Pray them as needed and pray them with feelings.

Eight
Pray as a Family

PRAYER IS INTIMATE. I believe that the family that prays together stays together. Family prayer time sets a good example for our children and teaches the entire family the importance of family unity.

As we progress on our prayer journey we develop prayer groups, prayer circles, prayer partners, and prayer links. These prayer relationships are part of our prayer family. On occasions, we will have a need to call in our prayer family. Those are times when two or more of God's children will come together in prayer to "lay hands" on the object of the prayer.

There will be situations and things in a family that take the brunt of our criticisms—"tick" us off, as we sometimes say. For many of us, multiple family members and situations have "rubbed" us wrong and "pushed" our buttons.

I will admit I am as dysfunctional and dramatic as the next person. But I do take time out long enough to own my actions and ask for forgiveness. My husband still argues with me about things I supposedly done years ago that were unacceptable to him! He honestly believes that our life together would be different had I not made certain personal life changing decisions.

Family gatherings are ripe for egos to clash. And Thanksgiving and Christmas get-togethers are where a collection of egos meet to express their resentments, jealousy, hate and every unloving emotion one can imagine. I say be prepared to address your own ego in a positive way. Close off your heart to other people's big egos, small egos, toxic egos and limited egos. Break free; don't be contaminated by other people's egos. I have learnt not to entertain a "little bit" of someone's ego in my life because when I do, the situation snowballs and gets bigger.

Some people find it difficult to accept that after a certain point, their arguments about past illusions just go around and around, and before long become useless blabber. It is even more difficult if you are that person and you are forced to admit that reality.

Having the prayerful support and confidence of your family is crucial in any relationship. Such mutual support makes it easier for one or the other partner or family member to succeed within a loving relationship. It may be a lot harder and less spiritual for some of us to be supportive when one individual is moving ahead at a faster pace. Be aware, ego is always active in our life and ego will never be loving and supportive towards anyone else.

You know by now that the person who pushes my button the most is my spouse. Understand that he and I have been together all of our adult life and we both feel that it is our right to be our authentic selves towards each other without having to apologize.

Imagine seeing yourself in a mirror that constantly shows you not to your liking. That is how it is with my husband and me. He forces me to face my dysfunctional self and helps me to make adjustments to the stuff that is not right about me.

Very often I let go of my need to be right so as not to make him wrong and I admit to him that we are both right in our desire to be loved and respected but we are both wrong to lay blame on each other.

The same is true in dealing with family members, friends, and those who will be disloyal and even betray us. We may want to turn the other cheek or "bless them" but our ego do not stand for such nonsense. Our ego encourages us to approach from a position of anger and fear on the premise that we are defending ourselves.

> *"When you accept who you really are, your arguments with others cease. For you no longer do battle with their personae. You see the light behind the mask. Your light and their light is all that matter,"*
> *Paul Ferinni.*

Getting angry at other people temporarily makes us feel better about the situation, but later our fear and guilt returns and leaves us feeling terrible. We ought to begin by giving up the need to make someone wrong in order for us to be right.

Carlos Castaneda, in his description and account of teachings from his spiritualist, Don Juan Matus, quoted Don Juan as follows:

> *To be angry at people means that one considers their acts to be important. It is imperative to cease to feel that way. The acts of men cannot be important enough to offset our only viable alternative: our unchangeable encounter with infinity.*

When we acknowledge and forgive our faults and our imperfections we are able to forgive others, whoever they may be.

Most difficult is the fact that I had to be willing to acknowledge my narrow-mindedness. I knew it would be impossible for me to grow spiritually unless I surrendered pent-up anger, haste to judge and unwillingness to forgive.

Always focus on your spiritual evolution and the role of prayer in your day-to-day living. To be honest, our emphasis should be on our experiences and how we kept on trying with prayer as our main stay.

> "This is my commandment, that ye love one an-
> other, as I have loved you," John 15:12.

Nine
Pray Without Ceasing

"Regarding my actual daily practice, I spend, at the very least, five and a half hours per day in prayer, meditation, and study. On top of this, I also pray whenever I can during odd moments of the day, for example: over meals and while traveling. In this last case, I have three main reasons for doing so: first, it contributes towards fulfillment of my daily duty; second it helps to pass the time productively; third, it assuages fear! I see no distinction between religious practice and daily life." The Dalai Lama.

I AM NOT SUGGESTING daily practices similar to His Holiness, the Dalai Lama. Five and a half hours of prayers and rites each day may not be practical for most of us. However, I was fascinated that His Holiness prays while travelling to "pass the time productively". And he acknowledges that prayer "assuages fear!". I interpret this to mean that prayer takes on fear, which suggests His Holiness has his own fears.

As I go about my business throughout the day. I practice periods of silent prayers and quiet affirmations. I must admit it is not an easy task to still my own internal chatter let alone the unwanted barrage of external noises, but with practice I am able. I am suggesting that after we pray, we wait in quiet meditation for answers. And if we don't think we got an answer that *IS* the answer.

Another practice that keeps me centered is my habit of refraining from speaking and acting if I am not ready to speak well of another person. By refusing to play the game of blame and shame I am able to defuse the ego's need for me to be unloving in that moment.

Those closest to you may express annoyance at your non-judgment and you could be the target of their subtle taunting snicker. Know that this experience is the attempt of other people's ego, which by the way, is always in play, to influence your response. Be aware; guard your spirit from other people's ego.

A life of prayerfully trusting in God often feels empty and even silent, especially if the folks around you do not believe as you do spiritually. But empty spaces are where God is. Empty spaces are where we should be sitting until our ears begin to hear.

During my periods of doing nothing, I feel lazy. The doing nothing times require me to accept my circumstances and go with the flow of my life. Those are the times when I suspend everything I believe to be right and trust in God's Grace to see me through my state of affairs.

Know that when we seek Divine relief during our weakest moments—the moments when we display hate, jealousy, fear doubt, anger—those unloving moments when our ego calls attention to self; we are, in fact, prayerfully asking God to show us a better path to return to caring ways.

> " Seek ye me and ye shall live," Amos 5:4

> "But if from thence thou shalt seek the Lord thy God, thou shalt find him, if thou seek him with all thy heart and with all thy soul," Deuteronomy 4:29-31.

"When thou sadist, Seek ye my face; my heart said unto thee, Thy face, Lord will seek," Psalms 27:9.

I know of someone who likes to complain to others about the things that bother him. And the more you indulge his complaints, the more unpleasant and passionate his story gets.

When the need is great and you are moved to tell someone about your worries refer to the following:

> *"...Whatsoever things are true, whatsoever things are honest, whatsoever things are just, whatsoever things are pure, whatsoever things are lovely whatsoever things are of good report; if there be any virtue, and if there be any praise, think on these things," Philippians 4:8.*

One of my favorite affirmations is: I am *"A Special Enterprise on the part of God"*—a direct quote by metaphysician Dr. Emmet Fox during a lecture that was attended by Mildred Mann (1904-1971) and mentioned in her book *How to find your Real Self*.

Each of us *"is a special enterprise on the part of God"*. We were born equipped with everything we need to grow and survive, physically and spiritually...we fit into God's plan. But we spend a lot of time in a busy state, doing things our way and so we never truly experience our role in the plan.

When I get to the place where life forces me to give up control about what I think an outcome should be I am inclined to tie an imaginary knot, hang on and wait for better days. And that may not be a bad idea if we believe better days are on the horizon. Regardless, when you are feeling hopeless, tie the imaginary knot anyway and hold on in faith.

> *"And call upon me in the day of trouble; I will deliver thee, and thou shalt glorify me," Psalms 50:15.*

It is difficult to let go and allow Spirit to guide. We usually have to be stuck with no way out before we turn our attention inwards. At that place, when we let go God shows us the pathway to victory.

Once we become familiar with our place of sanctuary; our place where we go for rest, then we should endeavor to go there often. That place is where we receive answers, guidance and the unconditional love we crave.

> *"For this cause I bow my knees unto the Father of our Lord Jesus Christ," Ephesians 3:14.*

My prayers are usually short. Your prayers can be as short or as long as you wish. Pray constantly. Pray for each other.

> *"I exhort therefore, that, first of all, supplications, prayers, intercessions, and giving of thanks, be made for all men," 1 Timothy 2:1.*

Develop your personal relationship with God. She knows your wants and your needs; She knows what is already your heart's desire. Go within and discover.

Most Merciful Father,
I thank you for who I am
I thank you for where I stand at this moment
I thank you for what I have become
Open my heart and mind to my purpose
Guide my steps in the right direction
Plant my feet on a perfect path
Make peace and love my friend
And compassion and giving my true companion
Let my soul rejoice and be glad
For Your Name sake
Amen

Ten

Go With the Flow

"And seek not ye what ye shall eat, or what ye shall drink, neither be ye of doubtful mind. For all these things do the nations of the world seek after: and your Father knoweth that ye have need of these things" Luke 12: 29

THE TERM "go with the flow" is one of those cliché phrases that can mean what we want it to mean. For me, "go with the flow" means I am willing to accept and go along with what is happening in my life in the moment—the good and the not so good. But is that the truth?

The truth is we are all living in a flow—life's flow.

Most people will go with the flow as long as they are in control of whatever is flowing. And since life happens with and without our participation, there will be times when we are required to stand still and observe.

Sometimes going with the flow means I am "standing still", doing nothing, with an imaginary tied knot. Those are times when I am overwhelmed with fear and I judge myself harshly for experiencing a rough flow. In those moments I give way to my *Built-in*

Prayer Mechanism.

When we acknowledge that the moment we are presently experiencing is likely different from moments past and moments to come, we will embrace life in the way it flows. We spend more time than is necessary stalled in the "Why me?" mode. To be honest, it is not such a bad thing to allow ourselves short-lived self-pity. But be careful that your self-pity moments do not lead you to extended dead ends. In those moments when you ask the "why me?" questions, allow your *Built-in Prayer Mechanism* to lead you to prayer solutions.

When life requires you to stand still, obey. Standing still when everything around us is moving at break neck speeds can be very frightening and quite often we find ourselves going with a kind of flow in order to avoid being trampled. Allow Spirit to carry you into calmer waters.

I must confess going with the flow has not always been easy for me. I am a control freak; I like to say I am the captain of my own ship; I leave nothing to chance. I feel real strong when I make right decisions, although I am first to beat up on myself when my decisions turn negative.

When we make up our minds to stop fighting our way through life; when we sincerely let go; when we give over all personal attachments and are flexible about outcomes, we know we are truly flowing with life.

Whatever the situation, your communication with the Divine, through prayers will keep you grounded and you will be alerted to move with life's flow when it becomes necessary. You see, God puts meaning into events that happen in our life, it is for us to be aware and participate.

Dear God,
I am weighed down by the flow of my life
I am bended and wobbly
I am weak and frightened
The waters are choppy, the sharks are circling
My ship is falling apart
Speak to the wind and rain
Still this storm that toss my life
Take control of this turbulence
Guide me to calmer waters
Steady my sails in this moment
Grant my request dear God
And give me a miracle
In Jesus Name I pray
Amen

Eleven
Surrender

I WAS MOVED by a burning desire to share the contents of my prayer journal. It occurred to me that we are a generation that is open to applying prayer as a solution to today's challenges. People are very much searching for positive changes in their life—seeking spiritual answers, if you will.

There are many who say they have no time for prayer, except when their own emergencies get pressing and they cry out in confusion and fear.

When our thinking is out of alignment with the core of who we are, things will fall out of place. Our prayers will hit sometimes and miss other times. We may find ourselves trying to force our way through unfamiliar cracks or just "hanging in there," as the saying goes.

Since life happens whether or not we participate, I say be there when things are happening around you, involve yourself with life. Hanging in there is not always the ideal way to go. See every moment in your life as new. We do not have to sweat our moments; we can make our moments short or long, happy or sad. We decide.

My understanding placed me on a path of continuous surrender. I found myself surrendering my former ways of thinking to a higher knowledge, although I must say, old thoughts and habits that formed part of who I am clung to me like Velcro.

I found out that new ways of thinking sometimes meant shaking core relationships. In the end, things and habits I thought I didn't need to surrender gave me no choice: they surrendered me.

My surrender demanded completeness, a process I know is likely to take a life time—my lifetime.

When we surrender to a situation we acknowledge that we are equipped to handle whatever the outcome may be. It means we have given over our state of affairs to a Higher Intelligence and we trust in that Higher Intelligence to bring all of our need in alignment with our true self for our good. In those moments of surrender; if you listen closely, you will hear: "*Wait on the lord; be of good courage, and he shall strengthen thine heart; wait, I say on the Lord.*" *Psalms 27:14.*

I often tell others to: go with the flow, cast your burden, surrender, let go and let God, and approach your day in compartments of moment. A friend said to me: "Enough of your moment philosophy, my negative moments have been with me for many years, I can't stand these moments no longer, and they are making me crazy." Regardless. I say, embrace the moment. If your moments are making you crazy then you are having a tantrum in the moment. Tantrums in any moment will grow and prolong your negative experiences.

To tell others that during their toughest and most difficult moments: all that they need to survive they already have, most likely would not be acceptable. Think about it, we are already sustained by God's breath of life and we are given free will; then all that is required of us is to surrender and be patient. It is true that we want to see instant display of progress but there usually is a bigger picture and God knows that bigger picture.

> *"Therefore take no thought, saying, what shall we eat or, what shall we drink, or whither shall we be clothed?" Read Matthew 6:25-34*

> *"Fear ye not, stand still and see the salvation of the lord. Which He will shew you today." Exodus 14:13.*

When I mess up I will admit that my management style is not working and I will cry out for Divine help:

Dear God,
This situation makes me feel helpless
I release my opinions
I relinquish my ideas
I lay down my human will
I put aside my human planning
I give up my human ambitions
I abandon my human pride and vanity
I now give this heavy burden to you, Father
I ask you to adjust and govern this situation
Take full control of the outcome and bless everyone involved
Amen

When I pray: *Take full control of the outcome, and bless everyone involved*, I am acknowledging that I can do nothing to make the situation better. I am relinquishing the circumstances to a higher power to bring the outcome to a satisfactory conclusion. I am giving up control knowing that all I need to do is claim God's power to make the situation right. I have put aside all doubt and fear and I am waiting patiently for my good.

How you are called to surrender is a personal matter. However, if your calling requires that you be a healer, a teacher, a preacher or a comforter, then it is unlikely that you will remain anonymous because your good works will be noticeable.

When you surrender to the Spirit within, your personal enlightenment journey is just beginning. You will be inspired to seek out knowledge and understanding. Divine energies that lie dormant within you rise to reveal the things you need to know. Wisdom presents itself when you ask for guidance.

> *"It is written in the prophets; And they shall be all taught of God. Everyman therefore that hath heard and hath learned of the father cometh unto me." John 6:45.*

You will find that in your zeal to be right and proper you sometimes devise your own ways of right. You may even be motivated to impose your rightness on others. Don't feel bad, it is your ego trying to stay relevant. Ego is part of who we are; we just have to be aware of its presence and be prepared to control its urges.

Notice that your steps along the road to surrender become easier with spiritual movement. A certain sense of peace replaces thoughts of impending doom and love is what you begin to call yourself. Less and less, you feel the need to struggle through life; something inside of you knows that life can only be right. You have no airs about what you do; you do what you do, because that is the way you were called to do it. There is no pride, no prejudices.

Surrender allows us to change our thoughts concerning anything we do not like about ourselves; or will not accept in relation to what we are experiencing in that moment.

The song says, *"I Surrender, I surrender all, All to Jesus I surrender, I surrender all"*.

Twelve

Cast your Burden

"Cast thy burden upon the Lord, and he shall sustain thee: he shall never suffer the righteous to be moved." Psalms 55:22.

WE TEND TO carry around too much stuff. Fear, hate, jealousy, resentment are just some of the unnecessary stuff we lug with us through life. This stuff weighs us down and gets in the way of our progress.

Metaphysician Florence Scovel-Shinn, in her book *Your Word is Your Wand*, says: *"Cast your burden on the Christ within and go free."*

Most people feel deserving of prayers for healing, forgiveness, deliverance, loving relationships, a place to live and a positive change in their financial situation.

Finance is a major challenge for many yet we hesitate to admit openly that we have actually prayed for hard cash to show up in our life. No doubt, a lot of our daily needs could not have materialized without the use of money.

"No man can attract money if he despises it," Florence Scovel-Shinn.

Whether we come into a family inheritance, we are paid for our services or we win a lottery, money will always be a key ingredient to our existence. Money is what society demands as payment for services rendered.

Regardless of our economic status, there will be times when we need to go directly, in prayer, and ask for paths to open so that we can have additional sustaining cash. Belief in God to lead us to financial resources to adequately do His work and to assist us in maintaining our general wellbeing is the right thing to do.

And bear in mind that unless we request money by name and denomination, it is unlikely that the angels will return with the exact amounts required. First Timothy 6:15 tells us to trust *"in the living God, who giveth us richly all things to enjoy"*.

> *"Money is God in manifestation, as freedom from want and limitation, but it must always be kept in circulation and put to right uses". The Game of Life by Florence Scovel-Shinn.*

Our Heavenly Father in is not interested in making His children suffer for material blessings. Some of us choose to deny ourselves of so-called worldly possessions, while others prefer to live spiritually and prosperous. I believe there is nothing wrong with either scenario because God has promised to *"supply all of our needs, according to his riches in glory by Christ Jesus"*. *Philippians 4:19*. We should, however, be responsible in our requests and uses of monetary gifts.

> *"Be careful for nothing; but in everything by prayer and supplication with thanksgiving let your requests be made known unto God." Philippians 4:6.*

I have benefited from the following affirmation:

> *"God is the Source of my unfailing supply, and large*

sums of money come to me quickly, under Grace, in perfect ways." Florence Scovel-Shinn.

My attitude towards money is to request exactly the amount I need in the moment, for the purposes I need it, trusting at all times that the money will show up as requested. There may be times when our requests for money seem not to manifest on time. My response to such a situation is "God is never late".

Remember, God supports our honesty and integrity; He knows we would rather be hard-working, trustworthy and reliable.

I have been bothered by debts that I never thought I could re-pay. My mind would bobble and weave through crazy thoughts; my stomach would turn and knot for many days.

But I always opt for casting my burden of debt on the Christ within and claim another miracle in a perfect way.

The words of Scovel-Shinn: "*Cast your Burden on the Christ within and go free*" sounded to me, at first, like a cop out. I now understand that when you get to the place where you confidently "*Cast your burden on the Christ within and go free*" you have truly surrendered. No burden is too heavy or too light to hand over to the Almighty. Our Heavenly Father tells us in Matthew 11:30: "*For my yoke is easy and my burden is light.*"

The ego that shares our life literally works against us; it is our stumbling block, our worse nightmare. Ego constantly reminds us of our fears, insecurities, failures and every negative reason why a particular situation did not work in the past and will not work in the present.

Have faith as you cast your burden. See yourself manifesting all that you want and need to sustain your daily living. Never having to worry or having to give thought about how you will live from day to day is God's plan for us.

I have made an effort to rid myself of cravings for things I "must have"; those things that I believe I cannot live without.

I have seen evidence of God's gifts of love in my life in such perfect ways that I felt I had to reciprocate to the bearer of these gifts. It took me a long time to accept that God works in mysterious ways, and in every moment, He is using each of us as instruments of His unconditional love to help all of his children.

My practice of praying for everything I need strengthens my spiritual confidence as I proceed on my prayer journey.

Prayer helps me to interpret my challenges as learning experiences, lets me work through these challenges and makes me carry on regardless. We can therefore mitigate a lot of our suffering by accepting that challenges are, in fact, opportunities to "*Cast our burden on the Christ within and go Free.*" *Florence Scovel Shinn.*

Thirteen
Know that you Know

WHEN YOU EMERGE from praying feeling pleased and blissful, I say you know that you know. You know that the angels are singing on your behalf; you know that the universe opened it arms to you, you know that you are pointed towards your blessings; you know that your Father in Heaven is saying "This is my beloved". That's an awesome feeling of knowing.

Remember the times when your personal life seemed off line; when you tried very hard to fix things but the situation got worse. You knew you should have let go and allowed God, but you twisted and turned the outcomes to satisfy your ego and you continued to "hang in there". You said, "This too shall pass" but deep in your heart you did not believe the situation would go away anytime soon.

If you are like me, you sweat your prayers and shed tears that say "sympathize with me, please". No one likes to see those tears. Certainly not your Heavenly Mother. Your Heavenly Mother grants you favors when you approach the throne of grace boldly.

"Let us therefore come boldly unto the throne of grace

*that we may obtain mercy, and find grace to help in
time of need," Hebrews 5:16.*

When we approach the throne of grace with confidence, contentment and ease, knowing that all we need do is to ask and our requests will be granted, knowing that angels are at hand, waiting on our behalf then we know we are participating in the manifestation of unconditional love.

I am not saying that every day you will be bold. The ego always wants to stay relevant, but know that the throne never moves and your Heavenly Mother always beckons you to come.

Knowing that you know keeps you from fighting your way through life; knowing reminds all of us to go with life's flow. It is a lot better to acknowledge and participate in your knowing for it magnetizes your blessings and brings you to your good, in perfect ways.

When I forget that I know is when my ego takes over my thinking. It is when I am weighed down with fearful thoughts. Usually my negative thoughts correspond with my carelessness, and then I back up and allow my *Built-in Prayer Mechanism* to take over.

*"Know ye that the Lord He is God; it is he that hath
made us, and not we ourselves; we are his people,
and the sheep of his pasture. Enter into his gates
with thanksgiving, and into his courts with praise;
be thankful unto him, and bless his name. For the
Lord is good; his mercy is everlasting and his truth
endureth to all generations." Psalms 100:3-5.*

I am the first to acknowledge that I am a work in progress. Life's lessons take a lifetime to learn, that's just how it is in life's classroom. But as we learn, we teach others. We are all teachers in the school of life.

When I listen and observe other people's challenges, how they dealt with those challenges, how they persisted in faith, I am moved to pray for their deliverance.

A state of complete knowing is when you surrender all outcomes to the Divine and trust that everything will work for your good. When you know that you know, you can affirm your beliefs and make statements of fact with confidence. I have repeated the following affirmation many times:

"I am happy. I am healthy. I am loving. I am whole."

When you completely know, you feel you are in harmony with the flow of your life. You know you are worthy of abundance.

Knowing that you know should not be seen as arrogant or being overconfident, knowing is accepting as true that there is no need to fear an outcome. Knowing is affirming with total confidence, *"God is never late"*.

Fourteen
Angels Come to our Aid

THE FACT THAT Angels actually exist and they matter to us as human beings is awesome. Consider this; we are in the midst of great numbers of angels whose job is to support us in this life.

Renditions of angels take on human looks. We see illustrations of them with wings, halos above their heads and praying hands. I personally believe angels are intermediary spiritual beings and they share our world. I picture them to be good friends and neighbours. I associate them with the spirits of ancestors, hovering and protecting us from harm and danger.

Angels often manifest in familiar earthly forms as needed.

> *"And the Angel said unto them, fear not: for, behold, I bring you good tidings of great joy which shall be to all people..."Luke 2:9-14*

It is easy for me to accept the idea of guardian angels and that my own guardian angel is the spirit of my departed great grandmother.

I was sixteen-years-old.

I was in hospital, ill with malaria, lonely and fearful. I don't recall, but I must have been praying for company because one night, a woman came and sat at the foot of my bed. She told me I would get well and she stayed throughout the night. I knew she stayed the entire night, for every time I woke up, she was sitting in the same spot at the foot of my bed. The next morning I thanked my nurse for staying with me throughout the night but she said, to her knowledge, no one did.

> *"He shall cover thee with his feathers, and under his wings shall thou trust." Psalms 91.*

I have since told this story to my mother and grandmother and they believe my hospital visitor and comforter is the spirit of my departed great grandmother, my guardian angel.

Angels protect us.

> *"For He shall give His angels charge over thee, to keep thee in all they ways. They shall bear thee up in their hands, lest thou dash thy foot against a stone." Psalms 91:11, 12.*

Angels defend us.

> *"The angel of the Lord encampeth round about them that fear him, and deliver them." Psalms 34:7*

Angels Direct and guide us.

> *"Behold, I send an Angel before thee, to keep thee in thy way, and to bring thee into the place which I have prepared."*

Angels worship and praise God constantly.

> *"Praise ye Him, all His Angels; praise ye Him all His hosts." Psalms 148:2.*

Angels are at our service.

Once I was faced with a big challenge that caused me great fear. I prayed. Later, as I sat in quiet reflection, I heard a clear voice from within which said: "A host of Angels are standing by, waiting to take your side". A host? How many is a host? I asked. "Countless" was the reply.

God, our Heavenly Father, placed at our disposal countless angels. Just think, each and every one of us has a host of angels waiting to do our bidding.

We are never alone in our worries. Angels are always on call to assist us. This is very reassuring.

> *"Call on us now as your companion angels, and know that we think of you as our companion humans, here to grow with us in wisdom." Author Andrew Ramer,*

> *"Angels remind us of God's supernatural realm, the immense and awesome spiritual world. But our mindsets tend to be earthbound, taken up with the material world we can touch and see." Rev. Canon Donald M. Langdon- Toronto, Canada.*

And angels sing.

In 2001 my husband and I were vacationing in Nassau, Bahamas. We had gone out mid-morning to explore the shops. He was busy exploring while I sat in the piazza on a bench, watching people. Suddenly I heard my favorite morning prayer being sung. I turned to look and sitting next to me was a petite native girl, no more than twelve years old. She was singing my morning prayer:

> *Thank you for waking me this morning*
> *Thank you for giving me today*
> *Thank you for every new day dawning*
> *I'll be thanking you*

Now those of my readers who are from the baby boom generation know that no twelve year old in the Bahamas should be familiar with the lyrics of this song let alone being able to sing it in its entirety. (*Thank You*—Jack Fishman/Marty Schneider, sung in the 1960s by Petula Clark). I was in awe as I listened to her sing.

What moved this child whom I never saw before, in a country I was visiting for the first time, to sit beside me in particular, and to be singing my favorite morning prayer?

We all have our angel moments. Moments when unexplainable things happen that let us pause for a supernatural time out. Spirit reminds us in those moments that we are divinely connected.

My child angel in the Bahamas never spoke a word to me; she sang her song and left.

God demonstrates his love for us in mysterious and loving ways. All She asks us to do is to be on the look out for those moments and honor and respect them.

"Praise ye him, all his angels: praise ye him, all his hosts." Psalms *148:2.*

Dear God,
Thank you for waking me up this morning
Thank you for giving me today
Thank you for every new day that I see
Father I thank you
Thank you for every new sound that I hear
Thank you for the air I breathe
Thank you for soft morning dew drops
Thank you for warm sunlight
Thank you for food, shelter and clothing
Thank you for family and friends
Thank you for everyone who loves me
Thank you for a healthy, happy life
Thank you that I enjoy these blessings
Father I thank you
    Amen

Fifteen
Beliefs and Prayer

And he to whom worshipping is a window, to open but also to shut, has not yet visited the house of his soul whose windows are from dawn to dawn," Kahlil Gibran.

I ALWAYS WANTED to believe in someone on a spiritual level, a teacher, if you will, someone who I can see, hear and touch. But to believe in someone of that nature means I would be giving my own divine entitlement over to her. I would have to believe that she has got more of what I would like to have; I would have to believe that anyone who teaches know more.

I am prepared to say that everyone will know what they need to know, when they need to know. I say that because in my own life everything I need to know is made known to me at the right time. People and circumstances are placed in my path for my benefit. Teachers present themselves to teach. Instructors appear in the moment, to say what needs to be said, and do what needs to be done in order to stir what is already within.

I know whom I believe and I am persuaded that he is able to keep that which I have committed unto him against that day.

Most committed observers attend Church usually once per week and "call it a day" until the next time. Others engage in multiple daily rituals such as prayers, meditation fasting, and the like. Regardless, we live in a faith conscious world and in many countries, observing people have privilege to express their faith without reprisal

> *"For where two or three are gathered in my name,*
> *there am I in the midst of them," Matthew 18:20*

Church is where I go to experience a sense of oneness, in the company of my church family. Church enhances my spiritual growth and gives me a feeling of belonging. It is where I often find social expressions and camaraderie. But as I reflect on the role of religion in today's society, I have to say that many converts come away from their churches and places of worship with unrealistic expectations and false judgments.

Some modern churches are business oriented. These organizations need financial resources to sustain their operations. Those of us, who use churches for the services they offer such as outreach, spiritual guidance and physical healing, sometimes struggle with guilt about our gratitude and the extent of our compulsory contributions. Some of us give generously while others may not be able to give as much.

My attitude is to suspend all judgments about what others do inside and outside of their gathering community and give generously from the heart as often as possible.

I always express gratitude to bearers of my gifts and give thanks to God, the Giver of all gifts. When you give from the heart you are free from guilt and those daunting feelings of selfishness.

> *"Every man shall give as he is able, according to the*

blessings of the Lord thy God which he hath given thee." Read Deuteronomy 16:17.

Some religions put strong emphasis on sin and worthlessness; and the need for mankind to repent and be "saved" in order to enter the "Kingdom of God".

I often think about others of God's children who never had, and probably never will have access to a brand of doctrine or dogma. We may see them as unsophisticated residents in a far away place yet somehow they too are aware of the Mighty Source we call the Creator or God. They too have felt the presence of Spirit within. And yes, they too communicate and receive Divine guidance in their sojourn on earth. That's just the way life is. That is how we were created to function. It is Grace. It is our birthright. It is our *Built-in Prayer Mechanism* engaged. This mechanism propels us to extend toward the mighty unseen Force.

Today, we are still being taught that we carry the burden of original sin and so we spend most, if not all of our life trying to get right with God.

Our guilt and any fear we may have of punishment for sins should be seen for what it really is—schemes we no longer have to accept as true.

For me, acknowledging my brokenness is the right thing to do. In doing so, I am able to forgive myself and move forward in love. You see, no matter how competent we present ourselves or how well we bandage our broken parts, our wounds will fester and ooze at the most inopportune time. Guilt wounds, fear wounds, blame wounds; rages, hurts and betrayals will appear and blow our religious cover.

I am mindful that others have views that are different from my own, although with joy I share my thoughts, feelings and prayers. I am inspired by the following statement:

> *"There is no place where your loving presence and testimony to God's love is not needed. All are crying out for your loving words. All would drink from the cup that quench your thirst"* Paul Farrini.

Spirit is always in our presence.

> *"For where two or three are gathered in my name, there am I in the midst to them,"* Matthew 18:20.

Regardless of your sacred connection, pray always and when you pray, use words and phrases that you are familiar with, the words and phrases you use every day. Pray your thoughts.

The following prayers are from my prayer journal. I sincerely hope you will find my thoughts, suggestions and prayers comforting. I am suggesting you create your own prayer journal. Pray as short or as long as you wish.

As you pray your thoughts out loud, use the melodies from your favorite songs to sing your prayers.

Dear God,
Your Will be done today
Today is a blessed and beautiful day
I thank you for this perfect day
Miracles and wonderful surprises will manifest
And splendor and glory will be forever
Amen.

Have fun at prayer.

Sixteen
The Prayers

"Be thankful unto Him and bless His Name,"
Psalms 100:4

Dear God,
For shelter, food and clothing
For opening heavy doors
For making my way smooth
For making my path clear
For removing stumbling blocks
For guiding me over obstacles
I thank you
Amen.

Dear God,
Thank You for life that envelopes me
Thank You for Spirit that directs me
Thank You for angels that support and defend me
My heart is glad
My soul rejoices
I sing Your praise
I celebrate this moment with joy
Thank You Father that I am called by Your name
Amen.

Most Merciful Father,
Thank you for me
Thank you for where I stand at this moment
Show me to my purpose
Guide my steps in the right direction
Plant my feet on a perfect path
Make peace and love my friend
And compassion and giving my true companion
I am filled with joy
I am happy, happy, happy
Amen.

Dear God,
I thank you for awakening in me a higher understanding
Thank you for the awareness that I am all that I need
I enjoy the view from the rock upon which I stand
I call forth health, prosperity, completion and joy
I manifest my desires
I make use of my strength and courage
I turn away from things that are not of love
I celebrate the Spirit in me that creates my will
Let the gifts I give be acceptable to the receiver
For the kingdom, the power, and the glory are Yours
Forever
Amen.

Dear God,
Your Will be done today
Today is a blessed and beautiful day
I thank you for this perfect day
Miracles and wonderful surprises will manifest
And splendor and glory will be forever
Amen.

Dear God,
Thank You for guiding me through today's challenges
Thank You for directing me through murky waters
Thank You for shining a light on my pathway
Thank you for smoothing the twists and turns
Thank You for making things bright
I now repose in peaceful sleep
Lord wake me up to another successful day
In Jesus' name I pray
Amen.

"Enter into His gates with thanksgiving,"
Psalms 100:4

Dear God,

Thank you for my friends

My friends have shown me tremendous love

They support me in good and not-so-good times

They bless me with gifts I would not have asked for

Their love is nourishment in tough times

Father, I appreciate my friends for their generosity

Let me be a source of their happiness

Let me be as good a friend to them as they are to me

Bless their families

Supply their needs

May angels hover and protect all of my friends

And may my friends and I always be together

In Jesus' name

Amen.

"Make a joyful noise unto the Lord,"
Psalms 100:1

Dear God
Thank you for waking me up this morning
Thank you for giving me today
Thank you for every new day that I see
Thank you for every new sound that I hear
Thank you for the air I breathe
Thank you for soft morning dew drops
Thank you, for warm sunlight
Thank you for food, shelter and clothing
Thank you for family and friends
Thank you for everyone that loves me
Thank you for a healthy, happy life
Thank you that I enjoy these blessings
Father, I am very thankful
Amen.

Dear God,
Thank you for waking me this morning
Thank you for giving me another day
Thank you for such a pleasant sunrise
Father I am thankful
Thank you for all of life's grand beauty
Thank you for mountains, valleys and plains
Thank you for oceans, seas and rivers
Father I am thankful
Thank you for making my heart beat
Thank you for precious breath of life
Thank you for this body, soul and mind
Father I am thankful
Thank you for every door that is open
Thank you for every chance I take
Thank you for granting me Your favours
Father I am thankful
Amen.

Dear God of Love and Mercy,
I praise Your wonderful Name
I praise You in the morning
I praise You in the evening
I praise the beauty of Your creation
I praise Your gift of life
I sing songs of praises, day and night
I tell of You with joy
I worship You
You are God
You are Mighty
You are Worthy
Praise be to You God of all
Let everyone say, "Praise be to God"
Amen.

Dear God,
With joy and happiness I welcome the Sun
I embrace the snow, the wind and the rain
The earth provides my fruits and flowers
The grass beneath my feet is soft
How pleasant is the morning breeze
I salute Your creation with a smile
I rejoice in the beauty of life
I am happy, healthy, loving and whole
This moment is full of love
You are Mighty and Wonderful and I praise You
Forever and ever
Amen.

God of love and Mercy
Father of my fathers
Giver of life
Creator of all
I am grateful for Your goodness
Let me always sing
And let my melodies go far
I love You Lord
Your mercy is greater than I deserve
Let your Kingdom come in my Life
And Your will be done
Forever
Amen

Dear God,
Thank you that I am alive at this moment
I thank you that those I love are with me
I am happy and glad when I remember (names)
Thank you for the pleasure of friendship
Thank you for the love of my spouse
My soul sparkles at the thought of my family
May my days in this place be long and pleasing
And may I always enjoy health and wellness
In Jesus' name I pray
Amen.

Dear God,

Thank you that I am the vessel that held and

nurtured the life of your child who is my daughter

I thank You for making me your choice for

carrying this wonderful gift into this world

This gift that I love unconditionally

Guide, direct and protect her as her life takes form

Show her my faith

Show her my strength

Show her my life that she may learn from it

May she always put You ahead of all her undertakings

Bless her with long life

Keep her in perfect peace

This I ask in Jesus' name

Amen.

Most Merciful Father,
I cherish the birth I celebrate today
I bless your Spirit within this birth
I claim Your miracle of love
Wonderful and marvellous are you, Dear God
I am joyful and happy
I sing Your praise
In this most precious moment
It the birth of my grandchild
Amen

"His mercy is everlasting,"
Psalms 100:5

Dear God,
I am sitting in a lonely valley
Hemmed beneath a high mountain
This place is strange and uncomfortable
I cannot remember when or even how I got here
Shine a light in this cold and isolated place
Help me to find my way out
Give me the strength to endure as I claw my way to safety
I now cast this burden on the Christ within
And wait for my miracle
In Jesus name
Amen

Dear God,

I approach you at the door where you say "Come"

In this sacred and revered place I surrender all

I rest my weary body at Your feet

My lips are sealed in reverence

My heart is open, my mind is still

I release my weaknesses

And wait in this place of quiet

"For I know whom I have believed

And am persuaded that he is able

To keep that which I have committed unto

Him against that day," (To Timothy 1:12)

In Jesus' name I pray

Amen.

Dear God,
I give you the contents of my heart
Purify with fire that which is unclean
Cleanse and use that which is useable
Bless me with a happy, loving and prosperous life
Enclose me with joy and total bliss
My spirit salutes the holiness in other spirits
My arms reach out in comfort to other arms
Keep me in oneness with my divine purpose
As I remain in Your service
In Jesus' name I pray
Amen.

Dear God,
I come to You with a contrite heart
Forgive my pompous and heady ego
Pardon my controlling nature
I seek You in this quiet moment
With my head covered and my hands clasp
I bow in the silence of my heart
Bless my soul with continuous good
Feed my hunger, quench my thirst
Cover my vulnerability
Protect me from the cold
And give me my deserve
In Jesus' name I pray
Amen.

Dear God,
Set us down gently at this new place of residence
Settle our hearts and minds in perfect ways
Let us rejoice in the newness of our home
Let peace and happiness rein within these walls
And angels flutter from room to room
Let love flow out of our hearts for each other
Provide for us in our humbleness
Give us continuous flow of everything good
May the peace that passes our understanding
Keep our hearts and minds together
And bind us closer in this life and forever.
Amen.

Dear God,

I took a fall during my walk today

My tumble was soft and painless

And when I stood up

The effort was easy

Thank you Father for making my landing soft

Thank you that there were no scrapes or cuts

Thank you for making the rest of my walk effortless

And thank you that I arrived at my destination on time

May angels continue to guide my footsteps

And bring me safely to the end of every day

Amen.

Dear God,

I place my husband into your hands

He has been acting mean and complicated for no reason

Father, I know that my husband's attitude and actions
toward me are not my worries

Therefore I will respect and honour him

Help me to keep an open space in my heart for him

Use my life as an example to him

Awaken my husband from his complacency and bring
him in harmony with his good

Please forgive his foolishness

In Jesus' name I pray

Amen.

Dear God,
Please forgive my impatience towards my Husband
I confess that I am angry, resentful, unloving,
Disrespectful and very unforgiving towards him today
Take this unkindness from me and give me gentleness
Let me rise above my old negative emotions
Let me see my husband as your child in need of love
Make me a good friend, companion and help-mate
I now release all negativity towards my husband
And cast this burden on Christ within and go free
Amen.

Dear God,
My heart is vexed
I do not want to pray for my husband
He pushed my button today
I come to confess the anger, hurt, disappointment
and resentment that I feel towards him
Forgive me Father and cleanse my heart
Help me to let go of this destructive feeling,
'though I feel it is justified
Show me my errors and reveal to me the right way
Forgive us both our folly
Give us both a new loving attitude towards each other
Make me happy and loving in this negative moment
In Jesus' name
Amen.

"…It is He that hath made us,"
Psalms: 100: 3

Bless my son
Fill his mind with wisdom and understanding
Help him to make right and proper decisions for himself,
his family and whosoever seeks his advice
Make him be successful in all his undertakings
Show him how to plan for the future
Bless him with good health and long life
May he always be paid well for his work
And may his money not be lost or stolen
Guide and protect him as he goes about his business
And let everything that he does be done to the honor
and glory of Your Name
Amen.

Dearest and Most Merciful Father,
I place my grandchildren into your loving hands
and surrender them to your care and protection
May angels bear them up lest they fall and be hurt
May they serve you as they grow and mature
Let them be kind to each other
Let them love their neighbour
Let their ways be gentle
May they learn from my kindness
Bless them in their going out and coming in
Hear my prayer for I ask in Jesus' name
Amen.

Dear God,
Have mercy on my mother
She held me in her arms at birth
She nurtured me in my formative years
She gave me advice when I needed
I thank you for directing the role she played in my life
She is on her way to the place you prepared for her
Give me strength to support her on this journey
Make my actions an example for my children
Bless my mother
May angels watch over her and comfort her
In Jesus' name I pray
Amen.

Dear God,
I place my mother-in-law before you
I have loved her from the beginning
And I will love her to the end
Thank you for placing such a caring woman in my path
Thank you for making her a part of my life's journey
Bless her with more happy and healthy years
Her knees now ache, her sight is waning
Please, God, relieve her aches and pain
May her voice continues to be strong with Your praise
And may I always bless her as she has blessed me
 Have mercy upon my mother-in-law
For she is good
Amen.

"The Lord He is God,"
Psalms 18: 3

Heavenly Father,
Come to my aid at this moment
Rescue me from my enemies
They surround me
They come at me from all sides
Show me your mercy
Shelter me from the aggression of my foes
I am battered and tossed about
Fear has come upon me
Wrap me in your arms and defend me
Give me strength and courage, dear God
To stand up and face my challengers
Let me not be afraid for I trust in You
In Jesus' name I pray
Amen.

Dear God,
I put my trust in you
Let me never be ashamed
Let me never be disappointed
My enemies surround me like hungry sharks
They threaten me and they mock me
But in you, my God, I trust
Send Your most powerful angel to rescue me
Stand Your most powerful angel on guard at my Gate
Post Your most powerful angel until I am safe
For thine is the kingdom and the Power and the Glory
Forever
Amen.

Dear God,
Take care of me
For my enemies have descended upon me
They enclose me with hate in their hearts
They curse and speak evil against me
Come to my defense and rescue me
Remove my foes from out of my path
Let them stumble and fall
For they mean me no good
Let my enemies hang their heads in shame
Let them not be able to look at me
Shield and protect me
From their lies and evil
For I ask these mercies in the name of Jesus Christ
Amen.

Dear God,
Please protect my mind from lies and enemy thoughts
Help me to clearly hear your voice over any other
Shield me from misleading and destructive thinking
Where enemy thoughts are already in my mind
Help me to push them back by inviting the power of your
Divine Holy Spirit to cleanse my thinking
Protect my thoughts from doubt and confusion
So that I can make right and proper judgments
Have mercy upon me, dear God, and give me peace
I humbly ask these mercies
In Jesus' name
Amen.

Dear God,

I stand in your presence covered in dirt

My eyes are filled with dust from my own folly

I cannot see my way out of this mess

I cannot remember how I got this dirt on me

Guide me through this valley

Shake me loose and stand me up

Help me to grasp and understand my lessons

And make me glad once more

In Jesus' name I pray

Amen.

In the name of Jesus Christ
Remove this stumbling block from out of my way
Carry me over this mountain and through this valley
Lead me across this huge body of water
Give me strength to endure this crisis
Make courage my friend as I stand my ground
I call upon Angels to surround me
Take charge of this situation
And adjust it in a perfect way
Amen.

Dear God,

I am weighed down by the flow of my life

I am bended and wobbly

I am weak and frightened

The waters are choppy, the sharks are circling

My ship is falling apart

Speak to the wind and rain

Still this storm that toss my life

Take control of this turbulence

Guide me to calmer waters

Steady my sails in this moment

Grant my request dear God

And give me a miracle

In Jesus' name I pray

Amen.

"Know Ye,"
Psalms 100:3

Dear God,
This situation makes me feel helpless
I release my opinions
I relinquish my ideas
I lay down my human will
I put aside my human planning
I give up my human ambition
I abandon my human pride and vanity
I now give this heavy burden to you, Father
I ask you to adjust and govern this situation
Take full control of the outcome
And bless everyone involved
Amen.

Dear God,
Doubt and fear are bearing me down
Please forgive my doubts
Take away my fear
Overlook my shortcomings
Forgive me in these moments of unbelief.
Help me to triumph over my fear of (name them)
Give me courage to move through these trying times
Give me strength to endure
Lord, have mercy upon me
And give me Your peace
Amen.

Dear God,

I come before You in a state of confusion

I surrender my confusion

I come with doubt in my heart

I surrender my doubt

I come with pain

I surrender my pain

I surrender my desire to be in control of this situation

Dear God, guide me to my good

Help me to understand and live my truths

And when my feet are off the ground as they are today

Carry me to a place of safety

When I am strong again, plant my feet on solid ground

I ask these mercies in Jesus' name

Amen.

Dear God,
I am overcome with hopelessness
Take my hopelessness and show me light
I doubt
Take my doubt and renew my faith
Fear has come upon me
Take my fear and give me courage
I cannot control my jealousy
Take my jealousy and give me love
My mind is cluttered with confusion
Take this confusion and direct and guide me
Make me sing again
I cast my burden of hopelessness, doubt, fear, jealousy and confusion *on the Christ within and go free* *
Amen.

Florence Scovel Shin—Your Word is Your Wand.

Dear God,
I come for comfort
I feel tired
I feel abandoned
I feel unloved
I am too broken to feel Your presence
I am too weak to understand Your wisdom
I am too ashamed to ask for forgiveness
Take away these broken feelings and make me whole
Give me according to my understanding
Feed me in morsels that I can swallow
Give me in portions that I can digest
Return laughter to my saddened heart
Shine golden rays upon my path
Make me glad again
This I ask in Jesus' name
Amen.

"Come before His presence with singing,"
Psalms 100:2

Dear God,
I repose in Your presence
I relax in Your arms
With covered head and empty hands
I bare my soul before You
Fill me with your Peace
Ignite my spirit with newness
Send me forward with a song
I thank you for this moment
And praise you forever
In Jesus' name I pray
Amen.

Most Merciful Father,
This moment is filled with power
I feel the awesome presence of Spirit
Bless me
Put a new song in my heart
And send me on my way singing
In Jesus' name I pray
Amen.

Dear God,
Come into my heart
Come to my place of refuge
Come where my heart beats tell
Come where my joy is complete
Come where Your peace exceeds
Come where Your strength gives more
Come Holy Spirit, Come.
For I ask these mercies in Jesus' name
Amen.

Dear God,
Come into my heart this moment
Open my ears that I may hear what You hear
Touch my eyes that I may see what You see
Speak Your words into my words
Use my hands and feet for Your work
Use my feelings to express
Make my entire being an instrument of Your Love
Use me Lord, for Your goodness sake
Amen.

Dear God,
Direct me to my purpose
Show me to my dreams
Lead me to contentment
Fill me with loving emotions
Comfort me with sacred songs
Bless me
And grant me the desires of my heart
In Jesus' name I pray
Amen.

Father in Heaven,
I look to the future with joy
I look with optimism towards my light
Give me a new song
Let me raise my voice in a new chorus
As I climb higher
And grow stronger
Be merciful to me
For the Kingdom, the Power and the Glory are Yours
Forever and ever
Amen.

"...And into His courts with Praise,"
Psalms 100: 4

Dear God, our merciful Father,
Your sons and daughters approach
Your seat of mercy
We come to draw water from the well of life
and to eat of the bread of heaven
Nourish us until we are truly filled
Let your goodness flow
Bless our going out and our coming in
And give us your peace
"Oh give thanks unto the Lord; for He is good for his mercy endureth forever": Psalms 136
Amen.

God our Heavenly Father,
We give You thanks for this moment
Your sons and daughters have come together in love
For a meeting of our hearts and minds
Bind us in perfect harmony
Show us Your plan
Let everything we say and do be to Your honour and glory
We love You
We adore You
We honor Your presence
We sing Your praise
We thank you for Your goodness
At this moment of shared friendship and respect
Bless us all and grant us Your Peace
"Behold how good and how pleasant it is for brethren to dwell together in unity": Psalms 133:1
Amen.

"Serve the Lord with Gladness,"
Psalms: 100:2

Dear God,
Bless the work I perform
Bless my devotion and commitment to my superiors
May the work I do bring love, happiness,
Prosperity and fulfillment to those whom I serve
I pray that You be Lord over my life
Open doors of opportunity for me that no man can shut
Let me be like a tree planted that brings forth fruit
Give me a clear vision for the future
So that everything I do may be done in Your honour and
for Your glory by Your name
Amen.

Dear God,
I bring your presence with me to this workplace
In this place, I speak of your peace and love
Help me to remember that you preside over everything that
Is decided and done within these walls
Energize me with your truth as I perform my tasks
And when I feel burnt out, infuse me with your Spirit
May the work that I do in this place brings joy to everyone
Merciful Father, Help me to remain peaceful during
today's most stressful moments
This I ask in Jesus' name
Amen.

Dear God,
My tasks are plenty
My responsibilities are heavy
Show me a clearer and easier path
Guide me back when I go off course
Give me strength to go the distance
Grant to me full knowledge and understanding
That I may complete my tasks in perfect ways
Bless my coming in and my going out
Now and forever
Amen.

Dear God,
Thank you for the team with which I work
Through the assistance of my team my work is lighter
I pray for the well-being of every member of my team
Show them my sincerity
Open their eyes to recognize that I appreciate their work
And let them see that I do not feel superior
Father I pray for their success and prosperity
I pray for peace and harmony
I pray for complete fulfillment
Bless us all as we go forward
In Jesus' name
Amen.

Dear God,
I am overwhelmed by the extra work that I perform
The hours I work are very long
And my paycheck is not sufficient to sustain me
Father, please adjust this situation
Provide for my needs in a remarkable way
Give me strength to endure while I wait on you
Let my performance be pleasing to my superiors
For all work is God's work
I pray for those who feel the way I do
Help everyone to overcome and prosper
I ask these mercies in Jesus' name.
Amen.

Most merciful God,
I spent many hours preparing for this interview
Help me to approach my interviewers with confidence
And let me respond in a positive way
Let your beauty be seen in me
Let everything I do, be right and proper
I release the outcome of this interview
I rest my burden at your feet
and patiently wait for my good
In Jesus' name
Amen.

Dear God,
Make me a blessing to all who come into my space
Use my eyes
Use my ears
Use my voice
Use my hands
Use my feet
Use my feelings
Use my potential
Use everything that I am, to do your work
And let everything I do be done to the honor and glory of your
Name
Amen.

Dear God,
Use me to bring comfort to others
Use the words I speak
Use my expressed feelings
Use my actions towards others to draw them to you
Let me say words that others need to hear
Let me do things that need to be done
Let your beauty be seen in me
And let everything I do be done to the honour
and glory of Your Name
Amen.

"We are His people,"
Psalms 100:3

Dear God,
Lord and Father of all
Teach me to be respectful of others
To be respectful of their traditions
To be respectful of their worship and praise
To be respectful of their language
To be respectful of their right to be different
To be respectful of Your Divine Spirit
Within each and every one of Your children
Give me an open and loving heart
To love as You love
And help me to be respectful of myself before
I ask others to be respectful of me
In Jesus' name, I pray
Amen.

Dear God,

Friend of the friendless, be the company I seek

When I feel lonely and abandoned

When others give up on me

When I am tempted to give up on myself

In times when my plans and efforts fail

When I become impatient and my cross irritates me

Help me to overcome my fear of loneliness

Let me trust in your friendship

This I ask in Jesus' name.

Amen.

Dear God,
Bless me with people who will understand me
People who will support me
People who will love me
People who will pray for me
Bless me with a community that will appreciate and love me
And when I experience joy
Bless me with people who will share my joy
Bless me with people who I can learn from
And most of all, bless me with a place to live where
nothing or no one will interfere with Your will for me
This I ask in Jesus' name
Amen.

"For the Lord is good,"
Psalms 100:5

Dear God,
I am standing in front of a huge door
The hinges are strong
The bolts are secure
I am hemmed in on both sides
My feet are wobbly
My hands are shaking
Give me strength and confidence
Show me a crack in this door
Boost me through an opening
And grant me the desires of my heart
In Jesus' name I pray
Amen.

Dear God,
You are the source of my unlimited supply
You know all my needs before I ask
In the name of Jesus Christ provide me with dollar bill
in every size, color and denomination, immediately
Make my wallet bulge with dollar bills and checks
Fill my wallet until it overflows
Grant my requests through your Grace, in perfect ways
And because I ask I must receive
Amen.

Dear God,
I am tormented by the fear of poverty
I fear that I am not competent financially
And I will not be able to sustain myself and my family
This fear is interfering with my logical thinking
And my ability to make right decisions
Help me to know only the fear of God
Give me courage to stand my ground
Let me trust in You alone
Dear God, hold my hand through this difficulty
And give me Your peace
Amen.

Dear God,

I awoke this morning short of money

My wallet is empty

Debt collectors are knocking

My faith is waning

Provide the money I need immediately, through Grace

That I may satisfy those I owe

Let not this temporary circumstance shame me

For I put my trust in You

I cast this burden of shortage of money *"on the Christ within and go free to have plenty"**

Amen.

* Florence Scovell Shinn–Your Word is Your Wand

"Because thy loving kindness is better than life,
my lips shall praise thee," Psalms 63:3

Be present at this table
Pour out your blessings on this place
Let Your Angels hover as we sit to eat
Bless everyone partaking of this meal
And bless the hands that lovingly prepared it
May we be nourished and our bones made strong
May Your healing power flow through our bodies
Let none of your children know hunger
And let them that thirst come to You
Heavenly Father, we praise you for this moment
In Jesus' name
Amen.

Merciful Father,
Let Your Spirit of love govern in the
 words I speak
Let me say words of encouragement at all times
Let my words build up and not tear down
Help me not to grumble and complain
Let me respect the rights of others
And seek to agree where there may be strife
"Let the words of my mouth, and the meditation of my heart, be acceptable in thy sight O Lord, my strength and my redeemer," Psalms 19:14
Amen.

"And Bless His Name,"
Psalms 100:4

Dear God,
I pray that in all my travels
You will reveal Yourself to me
As I pass through cities and towns
And move from place to place
Guide and protect me on every leg of my journey
When I stop along the way
To gaze at Your wonderful creation
And to marvel at Your greatness
Let me see You in all faces
Let me hear You in all voices
Let me feel You with every touch
Thank You Father for the gift of time
For as long as time is on my side
I will seize every moment to feel closer to You
In Jesus' name I pray
Amen.

Father,
Light my candle O God
Stand my light upon a rock
Set my sights on high places
Make clear my way I ask You
Hold me up with Your powerful hand
Plant my feet that I stand firm
I love You, I worship You, and I adore You
I praise You Lord, the Rock of my salvation
For Yours is the Kingdom and the Power and the Glory
Forever
Amen.

"And His truth endureth,"
Psalms 100:5

Dear God,
I lift up my friend Helen
And place her on Your healing alter
Wrap Your protective arms around her
Cleanse her body from cancer and make her well again
Heal her for Your Name sake
Give her more years to complete earthly business
May angels care for her and comfort her
I pray for others of Your children with cancer
With heart disease, high blood pressure, and every dis-ease that
makes Your children unhealthy
Father, in the Name of Jesus Christ
Heal Your ailing children and make them whole
Amen.

Heavenly Father,
I lift (name) in prayer
The body of (name) is in a state of dis-ease
Bring healing to the body of (name)
Make (name) well once more so that he/she may
complete unfinished business
I beg you Father restore the health of (name)
And make (name) whole
In Jesus' name I pray
Amen.

Dear God,
I feel the pain of your ailing children
I hear their loved ones praying for time
I hear cries for their healing
I see their tears
Father, I ask you to heal the bodies of Your children
Give them strength to endure, while their bodies
return to a healthy state
May angels nurse them back to perfect health
And give them a long and happy life
For I ask these mercies in Jesus' name
Amen.

Dear God,
I come to You with aches and pains
These pains are interfering with my daily living
Heal me Thou Great Physician
Touch the painful parts of my body
Relieve me of the hurts that cause me not to sleep
Restore my health and put me at ease
For this I pray
Amen.

Heavenly Father,
I am sad that (Name) has passed on
I miss our laughter
I miss the good times we shared
I will always celebrate the love we had
Thank you that you "go to prepare a place"
In my preparation to meet (Name) in that place
I ask you to bless me with quality of life
Make my memories of (name) be long and clear
Father, keep me in perfect peace while my mind is stayed on You
May the soul of (Name) rest in peace
In Jesus' name I pray
Amen.

Dear God,
I feel the pain of victims of war
I feel as one with those who lost to terror
I feel as one with mothers who weep
I feel as one with wives who pray
Bring peace to warring places
Change the hearts of warring peoples
Adjust their need to be right and perfect
Lead your children to Your light
Save our world for Your goodness sake
And give us total peace
This I ask in Jesus' name
Amen.

Dear God,
The drums of wars beat louder
Your children cry from the East,
the West, the North and the South
Your sons and daughters mourn
The heartless watch their destruction
Turn the minds of evil away from their acts
Rescue Your children
Pluck the souls of your children from untimely death
End all wars and bring peace into the hearts of mankind
For all Power and Glory are Yours
Now and Forever
Amen.

Dear God,
I pray for leaders throughout the world
Bless them with wisdom
Protect them from dangers of every kind
Let their leadership not be for self
Direct them to share their wealth with the poor and needy
Let their actions be right and proper
And everything that they do be to the honour and
glory of your Name
Amen.

Seventeen
My Truth

Say not, "I have found the truth," but rather,
"I have found a truth," Kahlil Gibran.

DURING THE WRITING of these pages I was prompted to "express your truth". What is this truth I am pressed to express?

My truth is my authentic self: it is the opposite of a fib, a lie and every falsehood I ever engaged. My truth supersedes any doctrine, dogma or belief that was ever shown to me.

My truth is the mighty Force within me; it is my spiritual opinion, my commitment to self, my courage to persevere and my willingness to soldier on in spite of my ego-based fear. My truth is my reason, my intention, if you will. My own truth is the one thing that brings me back to centre.

Some call truth their purpose, others call it God's purpose for them. Famous metaphysician Florence Scovel-Shinn calls truth "The Divine Design" for our life.

The moment you wake up to the "thing" that you love to do, the talent that brings you joy, the skill that you work at twenty-four-seven, and then give it away with affection and love, then you know you have found your truth.

I have heard it said that you know you're living your truth when you do what you do with ethics such as compassion, peace, love, patience and all those great traits. And, in fact, those are wonderful human qualities.

One way to recognize your truth is to inquire from within whether your true purpose is reflective of how you live in the present moment.

Know that each of God's children is meant to express his truth as it was designed from the beginning of time. When we realize our personal truth we will want to share it; our light will shine through from within, with very little effort on our part.

> *"Let your light so shine before men, that they may see your good works, and glory your Father which is in heaven." Matthew 5:16*

In many of my prayers I asked God to use me to express His love. Whereas I probably will never be perfect in my practice of the principles of the Prayers of St. Francis, I am willing to give the philosophy a try.

I had no idea I was being called to give over my thoughts and prayers for this very purpose. And when we give our lives to be spiritually used we notice that new talents materialize, talents we never thought we had.

I changed my old perception about prayer for I no longer approach from a begging and pleading point of view, to a God who is far removed, a God who resides in "Heaven", a God who is waiting to punish me for my sins. I commune with God, my Creator with every breath that I take and ask for His Divine energy to be manifested through me for the good of everyone.

I knew my truth began to unfold when I was prompted to tell about my spiritual growth; I knew I had entered into an enlightened state when I could no longer hide my personal beliefs; I knew that the "Divine Design" for my life was taking form when I willingly gave up many "must have" in a state of surrender; I knew there was something happening in my understanding which was far more significant and greater than my human self.

I watched as my spiritual future took shape and I concluded that everything I had done, up to this point, is to my heart's desire.

> "But every man hath his proper gift of God, one after this manner and another after that..." 1Corinthians 7:7

I know I am connected to all that I need to truly manifest my truth. Teachers emerged as needed to teach, instructors showed up at the right time to coach and mentors presented themselves in appropriate places to counsel.

Knowledge and information comes through in spoken and written words to guide me along the way. My truth pops up in melodies and choruses. My truth allows me to give the love I want to receive. My truth is my desire to be all I can be for myself and for those I serve. My truth is in all the things I am called to be.

My truth and my purpose are one. My truth is my life experiences, my talents, my energies, personal relationships that I formed and how I am maintaining my spiritual and physical health. But all of these things are meaningless unless I am prepared to give them over for God's work.

It is comforting to know that I have no need to go through life carrying unnecessary burdensome stuff. It is with delight and a lot of self-confidence that I pack and un-pack stuff as I proceed on my journey.

Commitment to God's duties may not be a magnificent affair; you may not get noticed or become rich and famous. What is important is that you are fulfilling your "Divine Design". Everything that you do is enveloped in love.

Mine is a truth that calls me to extend my love and forgiveness to my sisters; to withhold judgment against my brothers; to relinquish my ego-base perceptions about others and to surrender all to divine will. My passion is empathy towards my sisters and brothers in a way that even I do not yet understand.

I consider how privileged I am to be a participant in the evolution of a universal outpouring of Spirit. I suspect that I, like others of God's children, am called to accomplish my "Divine Design" in a special way.

> *"Who hath saved us, and called us with a holy calling, not according to our works, but according to his own purpose and grace, which was given us in Christ Jesus before the world began." To Timothy 1:9*

> *"And we know that all things work for good to them that love God, to them who are the called according to his purpose." Roman 9:28.*

This book is not about my personal viewpoint. It is not about my doubts, fears, resentments and every negative thought that I entertained.

It is about my spiritual evolution. It is about encouraging others to begin to make small changes that will empower them in taking steps, moment by moment to guide then to a truthful path. It is about trying something different. It is about a beginning that stirs the heart that is open. It is about embracing your freedom to express the spiritual being that each of us truly symbolizes. It is about doing our life with purpose so that the mark we leave on time will be seen and understood by those who walk the path we walked.

Every challenge I faced grew me closer and deeper in my quest for spiritual knowledge. The moments when I felt unloved and abandoned, my faith would not let me doubt God's love for me. I have faith that She is in my midst working things out for my good.

I believe there is a place where each of us belongs, a role we were destined to fill. However, a great many of us will leave this life without evolving into our right and proper role. Our prayer should be for God to show us our purpose, and arouse the genius that is within each of us.

Always remember, you are your prayers. Your prayers will take you to higher spiritual heights and deeper spiritual depths. Your prayers are stirred by an urging from within that summons your *Build-in Prayer Mechanism.*

Prove the authenticity of your *Built-In Prayer Mechanism*; let it stir you to pray in every moment. Trust in your prayers to manifest the results you seek; ask to be awakened to a clearer understanding of your self.

May God Bless and keep you until we meet in prayer again.

Closing Prayer

We thank you for bringing us together in prayer
Thank you for the privilege to release our fears
Thank you for Your unconditional love
Thank you for Your Divine Holy Spirit within us
Thank you for friends and families we've met in Prayer
Strengthen each of us to face our challenges
Bring us to our personal place of sanctuary
And grant us Your Peace
We thank and praise You always
In Jesus' name
Amen.

Why worry when you can pray?

Bibliography

Castaneda, Carlos, The Wheel of Time, LaEidolona Press, 1998.

Farrini, Paul, I am the Door. Greenfield, M.A. Heartways Press. 1999.

Farrini, Paul, Love Without Conditions: Reflections of the Chris Mind, Greenfield, M.A. Heartways Press, 1994.

Gibran, Kahlid. The Prophet. New York. Alfred A. Knopf. 2002.

Hill, Napoleon, Think and Grow Rich, New York, NY. Ballantine Books, 1987.

His Holiness The Dalai Lama, The Path to Tranquality, New York, N.Y. Penguin Books. 1999.

His Holiness The Dalai Lama, Ethics for the New Millennium. New York, N.Y. Riverhead Books. 1999.

Kundtz, David, Quiet Mind, One-Minute Retreats from a Busy World. York Beech, M.E. Conari Press. 2000.

Langdon, Donald M. Rev. Canon, Sermon on Angels. 2007.

Mann, Mildred, How to Find Your Real Self. Donald Gordon Carty E-Book.

Martin, Barbara Y. with Moralitis, Dimitri Change Your Aura, Change your Life. Sunland, C.A. Spiritual Arts Institute. 2003.

Ramer, Andrew Angel Answers: a Joyful Guide to Creating Heaven on Earth. New York, NY. Simon & Schuster. 1995.

Scovel-Shinn, Florence, Your Word is Your Wand, DeVorss, 1978.

Scovel-Shinn, Florence, The Game of Life. London, England. Vermillion Books, 2005.

Vanzant, Iyanla, One Day My Soul Just Open Up. New York, N.Y. Fireside.1998.

Williamson, Marianne, Illuminata. New York, N.Y. Riverhead Books. 1995.

Wesley, Charles. 1707—1788. Gentle Jesus Meek and Mild

Jack Fishman/Marty Schneider "Thank You."

About the Author

Olive Rose Steele is wife, mother and grandmother. She is an avid community volunteer and motivator. Olive has written several published and unpublished poems and short stories. For this work, she has drawn on her life experiences to bring inspiration to others; her goal is to continue to produce more inspirational writings.

Olive resides with her husband in Ontario, Canada.

Order Form

Please forward _____copies of *And When We Pray*
   To: _____
   Address: _____
   _____

City: _____
Country: _____Code_____

Please forward _____copies of *And When We Pray*
   To: _____
   Address: _____
_____

City: _____
Country: _____Code_____

Please forward _____copies of *And When We Pray*
   To: _____
   Address: _____
_____

City: _____
Country: _____Code_____

Shipping: $4.00 for first item, $1.50 each additional item.
Send order to:

Blackwood
4 Robert Speck Parkway
Suite 1500, Mississauga
Ontario Canada
L4Z 1S1

Please allow 1-2 weeks for delivery.

Reader's Notes

Reader's Notes

Reader's Notes